ESPECIALLY FOR

....

FROM

....

DATE

....

Published by Barbour Publishing, Inc., P.O. Box 719, Uhrichsville, Ohio 44683, www.barbourbooks.com

Our mission is to publish and distribute inspirational products offering exceptional value and biblical encouragement to the masses.

Member of the
Evangelical Christian
Publishers Association

HOLIDAY RECIPES, INSPIRATION, AND IDEAS FOR A BLESSED SEASON ✳ HOLIDAY RECIPES, INSPIRATION, AND IDEAS FOR A BLESSED SEASON ✳ HOLIDAY RECIPES, INSPIRATION, AND IDEAS FOR A BLESSED SEASON

The Best of
CHRISTMAS
AT HOME
COOKBOOK

BARBOUR
PUBLISHING

*Small cheer and great
welcome make a merry feast.*

WILLIAM SHAKESPEARE

···✦ Contents ✦···

Festive Appetizers & Finger Foods

Christmas may be a day of feasting or of prayer, but always it will be a day of remembrance— a day in which we think of everything we have ever loved.
AUGUSTA E. RUNDEL

Cocktail Meatballs

1 pound ground beef
½ cup dry bread crumbs
⅓ minced onion
¼ cup milk
1 egg
1 tablespoon snipped
    parsley

1 teaspoon salt
⅛ teaspoon pepper
½ teaspoon Worcestershire
    sauce
¼ cup shortening
1 (12 ounce) bottle chili sauce
1 (10 ounce) jar grape jelly

In a large bowl, mix ground beef, bread crumbs, onion, milk, egg, parsley, salt, pepper, and Worcestershire sauce. Gently shape into 2-inch balls. In a large skillet, melt shortening. Add meatballs and cook until brown. Remove from skillet and drain. Heat chili sauce and jelly in skillet, stirring constantly until jelly is melted. Add meatballs and stir until thoroughly coated. Simmer uncovered for 30 minutes.

Broccoli Squares

2 (8 ounce) cans refrigerated
   crescent roll dough
2 (8 ounce) packages cream
   cheese, softened
1 cup mayonnaise
1 (1 ounce) package
   ranch dressing mix

1 head fresh broccoli, chopped
3 Roma (plum) tomatoes,
   chopped
1 cup cheddar cheese,
   shredded

Preheat oven to 375 degrees. Lightly grease a baking sheet.
Arrange crescent roll dough in 4 rectangles on baking sheet.
Bake in preheated oven for 12 minutes or until golden brown.
Remove from heat and allow to cool completely. In a medium
bowl, mix cream cheese, mayonnaise, and dry ranch dressing
mix. Spread evenly over crescent rolls. Sprinkle with broccoli
and tomatoes. Top with cheddar cheese and serve.

Cheesy Potato Skins

4 large potatoes
2 tablespoons butter
   or margarine,
   melted
1 cup shredded Colby-
   Monterey Jack or
   cheddar cheese

8 (½ cup) medium green
   onions, sliced
½ cup sour cream

Preheat oven to 375 degrees. Pierce potatoes to allow steam
to escape. Bake 60 to 75 minutes, or until potatoes are tender.
Let stand until cool enough to handle. Cut potatoes lengthwise
into fourths. Carefully scoop out some of the centers, leaving
¼-inch shells. Set oven control to broil. Place potato shells,
skin sides down, on rack in broiler pan. Brush skins with butter.
Broil potatoes with the tops 4 to 5 inches from heat for about
5 minutes, or until potatoes are crispy. Sprinkle cheese over
potatoes. Broil an additional 30 to 45 seconds, or until cheese is
melted. Serve hot with green onions and sour cream.

Sweet Potato Balls

1 (40 ounce) can sweet potatoes
¼ cup butter
1 pinch salt
3 cups corn flakes cereal, crushed
¾ cup maple syrup
10 large marshmallows

Preheat oven to 325 degrees. Grease a 9x13-inch baking dish. Drain sweet potatoes and place into large bowl. Mash potatoes and add butter; mix well. Add salt to taste. Roll mixture into 3-inch balls. Roll each ball in crushed cereal. Place balls in prepared baking dish. Pour maple syrup evenly over all balls. Bake for 40 minutes in preheated oven. For the last 15 minutes, place a marshmallow on each ball.

Cocktail Wieners

1 (10 ounce) jar chili sauce
1 small jar grape jelly
2 packages smoked cocktail wieners

Preheat oven to 350 degrees. In small saucepan, combine chili sauce and jelly. Heat until well blended. Place cocktail wieners in casserole dish. Pour jelly mixture over wieners. Bake for 15 to 20 minutes.

Bacon-Wrapped Hot Dogs

2 to 3 packages hot dogs
2 pounds bacon
Toothpicks
2 pounds brown sugar

* * * * *

Slice hot dogs into thirds. Cut bacon slices into thirds. Wrap each hot dog with a cut piece of bacon and hold in place with a toothpick. Place wrapped hot dogs into slow cooker until full. Pour brown sugar over hot dogs. Cook on low for 3 to 4 hours.

Sweet-n-Sour Cocktail Links

1 pound cocktail links
2 cups ketchup
2 tablespoons mustard

¾ cup orange juice
¾ cup brown sugar, packed
1 tablespoon onion, grated

In large skillet, combine cocktail links, ketchup, mustard, orange juice, brown sugar, and onion. Simmer over low heat for about 30 minutes. Serve hot.

Experience an Inspiring Christmas at Home. . . .

Give an anonymous gift to a family in need. A gift certificate for groceries, toys, a donation of money— the possibilities are endless. Let God receive all the praise and honor for your thoughtfulness.

Mushroom Stuffed Triangles

¼ pound fresh mushrooms,
   coarsely chopped
2 tablespoons minced
   fresh parsley
2 tablespoons minced onion
3 tablespoons butter, divided

1 (8 ounce) can refrigerated
   crescent roll dough
2½ tablespoons grated
   Parmesan cheese
2 tablespoons sesame seeds

Preheat oven to 375 degrees. In medium saucepan, over medium heat, cook mushrooms, parsley, and onion in 2 tablespoons butter until tender, stirring frequently. Drain and set aside. Separate dough into 4 rectangles. Cut each rectangle in half, forming 8 squares. Arrange the squares on large baking sheet. Place 1 tablespoon of mushroom mixture on each square. Top each mushroom-covered square with 1 teaspoon of Parmesan cheese. Fold squares into triangles. Melt remaining butter. Brush triangles with butter and sprinkle with sesame seeds. Bake in preheated oven for 10 to 15 minutes, or until triangles are golden brown. Serve warm.

Barbecued Chicken Wings

3 pounds chicken wings
1 clove garlic, crushed
Celery salt to taste
2 tablespoons butter, melted

1 tablespoon lemon juice
Pepper to taste
1 cup hot sauce

Preheat broiler or grill. Prepare chicken wings. Combine garlic, celery salt, butter, lemon juice, and pepper in a small bowl. Brush wings with this mixture. Arrange chicken wings on grill or in broiler and begin cooking them. Baste with hot sauce after first 5 minutes and every subsequent 5 minutes until wings are completely cooked.

Sausage Balls

½ pound fresh ground
   pork sausage
½ pound fresh ground
   spicy pork sausage

2 ounces processed
   cheese sauce
2 cups buttermilk biscuit mix

Preheat oven to 325 degrees. In medium bowl, combine regular sausage, spicy sausage, cheese sauce, and biscuit mix. Mix well and form into 1-inch balls. Place on cookie sheet. Bake 15 to 20 minutes.

For unto us a child is born, unto us a son is given: and the government shall be upon his shoulder: and his name shall be called Wonderful, Counsellor, the mighty God, the everlasting Father, the Prince of Peace.
ISAIAH 9:6 KJV

Stuffed Deviled Eggs

6 hard-boiled eggs, peeled
¼ cup mayonnaise
2 tablespoons bacon bits
2 teaspoons lemon juice
1½ teaspoons Worcestershire
  sauce

1 teaspoon mustard
¼ teaspoon salt
⅛ teaspoon pepper
Parsley
Paprika

Cut eggs in half lengthwise. Remove yolks and place them in a small bowl. Place sliced egg white halves on plate; set aside. Mash yolks with fork. Stir in mayonnaise, bacon bits, lemon juice, Worcestershire sauce, mustard, salt, and pepper. Fill egg white halves with egg yolk mixture, heaping it slightly. Garnish with parsley and paprika.

Deviled Eggs

6 eggs
Dash salt
1 teaspoon white vinegar
2 tablespoons mayonnaise

¼ teaspoon mustard
Salt and pepper to taste
1½ teaspoons paprika
2 leaves lettuce

Place eggs in a pot with 3 inches of water. Add a few dashes of salt. Bring water to boil and cook eggs for 10 to 15 minutes or until hard boiled. Drain eggs and place on a paper towel to cool. Once cool, peel and cut eggs in half lengthwise. Scoop out yolks. Place yolks in medium bowl and mash. Add vinegar, mayonnaise, mustard, salt, and pepper; stir until well blended. Carefully spoon egg yolk mixture into each egg. Sprinkle paprika over yolk mixture. Place on a bed of lettuce. Cool before serving.

Pecan Stuffed Mushrooms

20 medium-sized
   mushrooms
3 tablespoons butter,
   melted
3 ounces cream cheese,
   softened
2 tablespoons bacon,
   cooked and crumbled

1½ tablespoons
   chopped pecans
2 tablespoons Italian-
   style bread crumbs
2 teaspoons minced chives

Gently separate stems from mushroom caps. Brush mushroom caps with melted butter. Fill each cap with a mixture of cream cheese, bacon, pecans, bread crumbs, and chives. Broil stuffed mushrooms for 3 to 5 minutes. Serve hot.

Garlic Pickled Eggs

12 eggs
1 onion, sliced into rings
1 cup distilled white
    vinegar

1 cup water
¼ cup sugar
10 cloves garlic, peeled
Salt to taste

Place eggs in medium saucepan and cover with water. Bring water to a boil and immediately remove from heat. Cover and let eggs stand in hot water for 10 to 12 minutes. Remove from water, cool, and peel. Place eggs in a 1-quart jar with onions. In medium saucepan, add the vinegar, water, sugar, garlic, and salt. Bring to a boil, then remove from heat and allow to cool for 15 minutes. Pour vinegar mixture over eggs and cover. Refrigerate for at least one week before serving.

·⊰ Tomato Bacon Rolls ⊱·

8 slices bacon
1 tomato, chopped
½ onion, chopped
3 ounces mozzarella
    cheese, shredded
1 ounce Parmesan
    cheese, shredded

¼ cup mayonnaise
1 teaspoon dried basil
1 can refrigerated
    crescent roll dough

Preheat oven to 375 degrees. Cook bacon in skillet over medium heat until evenly browned. Drain bacon on paper towels. Crumble bacon into small pieces in medium mixing bowl. Add tomato, onion, cheese, mayonnaise, and basil; mix well. Unroll dough and place a spoonful of tomato mixture in center of each roll. Roll up each piece of dough with the mixture inside. Place on an ungreased baking sheet and bake in preheated oven for 11 to 14 minutes or until golden brown.

Chicken Quesadillas

1 tablespoon vegetable oil
1 skinless, boneless chicken
   breast, cut into strips
1 small onion, chopped

3 tablespoons salsa
10 (10 inch) flour tortillas
2 cups shredded Colby-
   Monterey Jack cheese

Preheat oven to 350 degrees. Spray cookie sheet with nonstick cooking spray. In large skillet, add vegetable oil. Fry chicken strips until they are no longer pink. Add onion and fry, stirring constantly. Add salsa; stir well. Place tortillas between two damp paper towels and microwave on high for 1 minute. Spread some of the chicken mixture over half the side of one tortilla. Sprinkle cheese over the mixture. Fold tortilla in half. Repeat with remaining tortillas. Arrange tortillas on prepared cookie sheet. Bake until cheese is melted. Cut quesadillas into fourths.

Cream Cheese Penguins

18 jumbo black olives, pitted
1 (8 ounce) package cream cheese, softened
1 carrot
18 small black olives

Cut a slit from top to bottom, lengthwise, into side of each jumbo olive. Carefully insert about 1 teaspoon of cream cheese into each olive. Slice carrot into eighteen ¼-inch-thick rounds; cut a small notch out of each carrot slice to form feet. Save the cutout pieces and press one into the center of each small olive to form the beak. If necessary, cut a small slit into each olive before inserting the beak. Set a jumbo olive, large hole side down, onto a carrot slice. Then set a small olive onto the large olive, adjusting so that beak, cream cheese chest, and notch in carrot slice line up. Secure with toothpick.

Parmesan Bread Sticks

1 (1 pound) loaf french bread
¾ cup margarine or butter, melted
¼ cup grated Parmesan cheese

Preheat oven to 425 degrees. Cut bread loaf into 5 pieces, each about 4 inches long. Cut each piece lengthwise into 6 sticks. After brushing sides with melted margarine and sprinkling with Parmesan cheese, place sticks on ungreased jelly roll pan and bake about 8 minutes, or until golden.

···❦ Cherry Tomato Blossoms ❦···

1 pint medium to large cherry tomatoes (about 24)
2 ounces cream cheese, cut into ½-inch cubes (about 24)
Parsley sprigs

Place tomatoes stem side down and cut each into fourths (almost through to bottom). Insert cheese cube in center of each tomato. Top with small parsley sprigs to garnish.

Experience an Inspiring Christmas at Home. . . .

Pick up some great Christmas gifts for your loved ones who enjoy cooking and baking. Measuring spoons and cups, spices, recipe cards, a recipe organizer, dish towels, and other fun kitchen gadgets are sure to please the family chef!

Mushrooms Stuffed with Crab

24 medium mushrooms
   (about 1 pound)
3 tablespoons butter or olive
   oil, divided
1 shallot, minced
1 (8 ounce) package cream
   cheese, softened

1 (6 ounce) can crabmeat
1 tablespoon lemon juice
1 tablespoon minced parsley
½ teaspoon prepared
   white horseradish
¼ teaspoon salt
Dash cayenne

Remove and finely chop stems of mushrooms. Melt 1 tablespoon butter in skillet over medium heat. Add shallot and mushroom stems and cook about 3 minutes, or until mushroom liquid has evaporated. Pour mixture into medium bowl and add cream cheese, crabmeat, lemon juice, parsley, horseradish, salt, and cayenne, blending well. Melt remaining butter in skillet over medium heat. Remove from heat and toss mushroom caps in skillet until well coated with butter. Place caps stem end up on baking sheet and fill with 2 teaspoons crab mixture. Bake 10 minutes, or until filling is bubbly and mushrooms are tender.

Salmon Party Ball

1 (8 ounce) package cream
   cheese, softened
1 (16 ounce) can salmon,
   drained and flaked
1 tablespoon finely
   chopped onion

1 tablespoon lemon juice
¼ teaspoon liquid smoke
¼ teaspoon salt
⅓ cup chopped nuts
¼ cup snipped parsley

Mix all ingredients except nuts and parsley. Shape mixture into ball. Cover and chill at least 8 hours. Coat ball with parsley and nut mixture.

This star drew nigh to the northwest,
O'er Bethlehem it took its rest;
And there it did both stop and stay,
Right over the place where Jesus lay.
TRADITIONAL ENGLISH CAROL

Hot Sausage and Cheese Puffs

1 pound hot or sweet Italian sausage
1 pound sharp cheddar cheese, shredded
3 cups biscuit baking mix
¾ cup water

Cook sausage, breaking up with fork until no longer pink.
Drain and cool completely. Combine sausage, cheese, baking
mix, and water. Mix with fork until just blended. Roll into 1-inch
balls and place on baking sheet. Bake at 400 degrees for 12 to
15 minutes.

Cucumbers Stuffed
with Feta Cheese

2 medium English (hothouse) cucumbers, scrubbed
1 (8 ounce) package cream cheese, softened
½ cup crumbled feta cheese
2 tablespoons chopped fresh dill or 2 teaspoons dried dill

Remove cucumber ends and cut in half lengthwise. Remove seeds from both halves with melon baller and set aside. Blend cream cheese, feta cheese, and dill until well mixed. Spoon cheese mixture into each cucumber half and reassemble halves, pressing together gently. Wrap in plastic wrap and chill. Before serving, cut into ½-inch slices.

Bacon Crispies

¾ cup butter, softened
1½ cups all-purpose flour
Salt and pepper to taste

½ cup grated cheddar cheese
6 ounces bacon, finely
  chopped and divided

Heat oven to 325 degrees. Beat butter, flour, salt, and pepper until smooth. Add grated cheese and ⅔ bacon and mix well. Drop by teaspoonfuls onto greased baking sheet, sprinkling with remaining bacon. Bake for 30 minutes or until lightly browned. Cool and store in airtight tin.

Experience an Inspiring Christmas at Home. . . .

Discover some old-fashioned holiday fun. Join a caroling group and visit local nursing homes and hospitals. Or just travel around the neighborhood spreading Christmas cheer. You'll brighten hearts as well as lift spirits (even if you do sing a little off-key!).

Miniature Ham Puffs

1 cup water
½ cup margarine or butter
1 cup all-purpose flour
4 eggs
3 (4.5 ounce) cans
  deviled ham

1 tablespoon horseradish
¾ teaspoon pepper
¾ teaspoon onion salt
⅓ cup dairy sour cream

Heat oven to 400 degrees. In saucepan, bring water and margarine to a rolling boil. Add flour and stir vigorously over low heat for about 1 minute, or until mixture forms a ball; remove from heat. Beat in eggs, all at once, until smooth and glossy. Drop dough by teaspoonfuls onto ungreased cookie sheet. Bake about 25 minutes, or until puffed, golden brown, and dry. Cool on wire racks. Mix deviled ham, horseradish, pepper, onion salt, and sour cream; chill. Just before serving, remove tops of puffs with sharp knife, scooping out any filaments of soft dough. Fill each puff with ham mixture.

⸙ Festive Nibbles ⸙

1 cup flour, plus extra
   for dusting
1 teaspoon mustard powder
2 pinches salt
½ cup butter, plus extra
   for greasing
3 ounces cheddar
   cheese, grated

Pinch cayenne
2 tablespoons water
1 egg, beaten and divided
Poppy seeds, sunflower
   seeds, or sesame
   seeds, to decorate

Sift together flour, mustard powder, and salt. Cut butter into mixture until it resembles fine bread crumbs. Stir in cheese and cayenne and sprinkle with water. Add half the beaten egg, mix to a firm dough, and knead lightly until smooth. Roll out dough on a lightly floured board. Cut out desired shapes and place on greased baking sheet, brushing tops with remaining egg. Sprinkle seeds over top to decorate and bake at 350 degrees for 10 minutes.

⟶ Chicken Bites ⟵

4 chicken breasts, boned and skinned
1 cup finely crushed round buttery crackers (about 24)
½ cup grated Parmesan cheese
¼ cup finely chopped walnuts

1 teaspoon dried thyme leaves
1 teaspoon dried basil leaves
½ teaspoon seasoned salt
¼ teaspoon pepper
½ cup margarine or butter, melted

Heat oven to 400 degrees. Place aluminum foil over 2 baking sheets. Cut chicken into 1-inch pieces. Combine cracker crumbs, Parmesan cheese, walnuts, thyme, basil, seasoned salt, and pepper. Dip chicken pieces into melted margarine, then into crumb mixture. Place chicken pieces on cookie sheets and bake uncovered for 20 to 25 minutes, or until golden brown.

Baked Water Chestnuts

1 can whole water chestnuts
½ cup soy sauce
Sugar
4 slices bacon, cut in half lengthwise and widthwise

* * * * * * * * * * *

Drain water chestnuts. Marinate in soy sauce for 30 minutes. Drain sauce from water chestnuts and roll each water chestnut in sugar. Wrap each chestnut in strip of bacon. Bake at 400 degrees for 30 minutes.

Blue Cheese–Stuffed Dates

2 ounces blue cheese
Milk
12 dried dates, pitted and cut in half lengthwise
24 blanched almonds, toasted
Dash cayenne pepper

In small bowl, mix cheese with hand mixer until creamy. Add a few drops of milk if cheese is too crumbly. Place dates on a serving platter. Spread about 1 teaspoon of cheese on the cut side of each date. Top with 1 almond. Sprinkle stuffed dates with a dash of cayenne pepper. Serve.

Born Thy
people to deliver,
Born a child and yet a King,
Born to reign in us forever,
Now Thy gracious
kingdom bring.
CHARLES WESLEY

Bruschetta

4 cups Roma tomatoes,
   chopped and seeded
1 medium onion, chopped
6 to 8 basil leaves, chopped
2 to 3 tablespoons fresh
   oregano, chopped

3 to 5 garlic cloves, minced
½ teaspoon black pepper
2 tablespoons olive oil
1 (16 ounce) loaf french
   bread, cut into 24 slices
Olive oil cooking spray

In a medium mixing bowl, combine tomatoes, onion, basil, oregano, garlic, black pepper, and olive oil. Cover and chill for 2 to 3 hours to blend flavors. When ready to serve, spray each bread slice with cooking spray and broil until lightly browned. Spoon mixture onto bread slices and serve.

When they saw the star, they were overjoyed. . . . They saw the child with his mother Mary, and they bowed down and worshiped him. Then they opened their treasures and presented him with gifts.
MATTHEW 2:10–11 NIV

Cheese and Chicken Empanadas

½ cup shredded Monterey
Jack cheese
½ cup shredded mild
cheddar cheese
1 cup shredded
cooked chicken
1 jalapeño pepper, diced
½ tablespoon minced
red onion

½ teaspoon ground cumin
½ teaspoon salt
2 frozen pie shells, thawed
3 egg yolks, lightly beaten
2 tablespoons coarse
kosher salt
1 tablespoon chili powder

In bowl, mix together cheeses, chicken, jalapeño, onion, cumin, and salt. Refrigerate until ready to assemble empanadas. On floured surface, roll out pie shells and cut into eight 4-inch circles. Use all dough by rerolling scraps. Place approximately 2 tablespoons of cheese and chicken mixture in center of each dough circle. Fold each circle in half and crimp edges with fork. Place on greased baking pan or cookie sheet and brush top of each empanada with egg yolk. Sprinkle top with kosher salt and chili powder. Bake at 400 degrees for 12 to 13 minutes. Serve warm or at room temperature.

Cheese Straws

½ cup butter, softened
1 pound shredded sharp cheddar cheese
½ teaspoon salt
1¾ cups flour
¼ teaspoon ground red pepper

In large bowl, cream butter. Add remaining ingredients and combine thoroughly. On floured surface, roll into ¼-inch-thick rectangle. Cut into narrow strips approximately 4 inches long. Bake at 350 degrees for 20 to 25 minutes.

⋅⋅❄ Cinnamon-Glazed Almonds ❄⋅⋅

1 egg white
1 teaspoon cold water
4 cups whole almonds
½ cup sugar
¼ teaspoon salt
½ teaspoon ground cinnamon

Lightly grease a 10x15-inch jelly roll pan. Lightly beat egg white. Add water and beat until frothy but not stiff. Place almonds in large bowl. Drizzle egg mixture over nuts and stir until well coated. In small bowl, combine sugar, salt, and cinnamon; sprinkle over nuts. Toss to coat, and spread evenly in prepared pan. Bake at 250 degrees for 45 minutes to 1 hour, stirring occasionally until golden. Allow to cool completely. Store almonds in airtight container.

❧ Debbie's Cheese Ball ❧

1 jar Old English
   cheese spread
1 jar Roka blue cheese spread
1 (8 ounce) package cream
   cheese, softened

1 small onion, minced
1 dash Worcestershire sauce
¾ cup chopped pecans

With a fork, thoroughly blend cheese spreads, cream cheese, onion, and Worcestershire sauce. Sprinkle chopped pecans onto sheet of waxed paper. Spoon cheese mixture onto pecans. Roll cheese mixture in pecans and form into ball. Wrap ball in plastic wrap and chill thoroughly before serving with crackers.

Experience an Inspiring
Christmas at Home. . . .

Choose one night a week during Advent to sit down with your family and read through a short devotional and then pray together. Hot cocoa afterward is a must!

⋯⊰ Ham Bites ⊱⋯

1 cup dry bread crumbs, divided
1 cup ground cooked ham
2 eggs, beaten
1½ cups (2 ounces) shredded sharp cheddar cheese
¼ cup grated onion
2 tablespoons brown sugar
1 tablespoon Dijon mustard
Vegetable oil

Combine ½ cup bread crumbs with all ground ham, eggs, shredded cheese, onion, brown sugar, and mustard in large bowl. Mix well. Form ham mixture into 1-inch balls. Roll balls in remaining ½ cup bread crumbs, pressing firmly so crumbs adhere. Cover and refrigerate ham balls until chilled thoroughly. Heat vegetable oil to 375 degrees and deep fry ham balls for 1 to 2 minutes or until golden brown. Drain on paper towels. Serve immediately with barbecue sauce, honey mustard, or other favorite dipping sauces.

Holiday Cheese Ring

4 cups shredded sharp cheddar cheese
1 cup finely chopped pecans
1 cup mayonnaise
1 small onion, finely chopped
1 pinch black pepper
1 pinch cayenne pepper
1 dash Worcestershire sauce
1 jar strawberry or raspberry preserves

In mixing bowl, blend together all ingredients except preserves. Spoon mixture into greased gelatin ring mold. Refrigerate for 3 to 4 hours. Transfer cheese ring from mold to serving plate. Spoon preserves into center of ring. Serve with crackers.

Hot Crab Dip

1 (8 ounce) package cream cheese, softened
½ teaspoon prepared horseradish
2 tablespoons minced green onions
1 tablespoon Worcestershire sauce
1 (6.5 ounce) can crabmeat, drained
⅓ cup slivered almonds
Paprika

In mixing bowl, blend together cream cheese, horseradish, onions, Worcestershire sauce, and crabmeat. Spread into 3-cup baking dish. Sprinkle with almonds, then with paprika. Bake at 350 degrees for 30 minutes. Serve with wheat or rye crackers.

Hot Ryes

1 cup finely grated swiss cheese
¼ cup cooked and crumbled bacon
1 (4.5 ounce) can chopped black olives
¼ cup minced onion
1 teaspoon Worcestershire sauce
¼ cup mayonnaise
1 loaf party rye bread, sliced

Mix first six ingredients together. Spread 2 to 3 teaspoons of mixture on each slice of bread. Bake at 375 degrees for 10 to 15 minutes or until bubbly.

Piglets-in-a-Blanket

1 (10 count) can refrigerator biscuits
20 cocktail sausages

Cut each biscuit in half and wrap each half around a sausage.
Place on ungreased cookie sheet and bake at 400 degrees for 8
to 10 minutes or until biscuits are lightly browned. Serve with
favorite dipping sauces.

Experience an Inspiring Christmas at Home. . . .

*Create a festive atmosphere in your dining
room by hanging stockings on all the chairs.
A week before Christmas, begin leaving
small gifts or heartfelt notes in the stockings.
Your family will be reminded of how
special they are to you.*

⋯⋖ Sausage and Apple Bites ⋗⋯

2½ cups baking mix
1 pound mild breakfast sausage
1½ cups shredded sharp cheddar cheese
¼ cup finely chopped celery
2 tablespoons minced onion
1 pinch garlic powder
2 medium tart apples, finely chopped

In mixing bowl, combine all ingredients; knead until well blended. Roll into 1-inch balls and place on greased cookie sheet. Bake at 350 degrees for 15 to 20 minutes or until browned, turning each ball after 10 minutes.

Bountiful Beverages

Good news from
heaven the angels bring,
Glad tidings to the earth they sing:
To us this day a child is given,
To crown us with the
joy of heaven.
MARTIN LUTHER

Best Eggnog

6 fresh eggs, beaten well
1 (14 ounce) can sweetened condensed milk
Pinch salt
1 teaspoon vanilla extract
1 quart milk
⅔ cup heavy whipping cream
Nutmeg, if desired

In large mixing bowl, beat eggs until thick and smooth. Blend in condensed milk, salt, and vanilla; slowly add milk. In small bowl, beat whipping cream until peaks start to form; then use a spatula to fold it into the egg mixture. Serve chilled. Servings may be sprinkled with nutmeg. Note: Please make your guests aware of the use of raw eggs.

Christmas Morning Coffee

1 pot (10 cups) brewed coffee
⅓ cup water
½ cup sugar
¼ cup unsweetened cocoa
¼ teaspoon ground cinnamon
Pinch grated nutmeg
Sweetened whipped topping, if desired

Prepare coffee. While coffee is brewing, heat water to a low boil in large saucepan. Stir in sugar, cocoa, cinnamon, and nutmeg. Bring back to a low boil for 1 minute, stirring occasionally. Combine coffee with cocoa mixture in saucepan. To serve, pour into mugs and top with sweetened whipped topping if desired.

·•❧ Christmas Tea Mix ❧•·

1 cup instant tea mix
2 cups powdered
    orange drink mix
3 cups sugar

½ cup red cinnamon candies
½ teaspoon ground cloves
1 envelope lemonade mix

Mix ingredients and store in airtight container. To prepare one serving, add 1 heaping teaspoon to 1 cup hot water.

Dear Lord, help me to keep my eyes fixed on You throughout the Christmas season. When the commercialism of the holiday threatens to snuff out the real meaning of Christmas in my heart, remind me of the Gift of Hope You sent on that silent night so long ago. Amen.

Creamy Orange Drink

6 cups orange juice, divided
1 teaspoon vanilla extract
1 (3.4 ounce) package instant vanilla pudding
1 envelope whipped topping mix

In a large mixing bowl, combine half of orange juice with vanilla, pudding mix, and whipped topping mix. Beat until smooth; then mix in remaining juice. Chill thoroughly.

Green Christmas Punch

2 envelopes lemon-lime drink mix
1½ cups sugar
2 quarts water
1 (20 ounce) can pineapple juice
1 (2 liter) bottle ginger ale
½ gallon lime sherbet
Maraschino cherries, if desired

Dissolve drink mix and sugar in water. Stir in pineapple juice. Chill. To serve, blend lemon-lime mixture with ginger ale in punch bowl. Scoop lime sherbet into punch bowl. If desired, place a maraschino cherry on each scoop of sherbet.

Fireside Mocha Mix

2 cups nondairy coffee creamer
1½ cups instant coffee mix
1½ cups hot cocoa mix
1½ cups sugar
1 teaspoon ground cinnamon
¼ teaspoon ground nutmeg

In large bowl, combine all ingredients. Store mixture in airtight
container. To prepare one serving, stir 2 heaping tablespoons
of mix into 1 cup boiling water.

Festive Holiday Punch

8 cups apple juice
8 cups cranberry juice cocktail
2 red apples, sliced
2 cups cranberries
3 liters lemon-lime soda
Ice cubes as needed

Combine apple and cranberry juices in punch bowl. Fifteen minutes before serving, add apple slices, cranberries, soda, and ice cubes. Do not stir.

···❦ Holiday Punch ❧···

1 (3 ounce) package cherry gelatin
1 cup boiling water
1 (6 ounce) can frozen lemonade concentrate
3 cups cold water
1 quart cranberry juice
Ice cubes
1 (12 ounce) can ginger ale

Dissolve gelatin completely in boiling water. Stir in lemonade concentrate, cold water, and cranberry juice. Chill. Immediately before serving, pour mixture over ice cubes in large punch bowl. Stir in ginger ale.

Hot Vanilla

4 cups milk
4 teaspoons honey
½ teaspoon vanilla extract
Ground cinnamon

In a saucepan, heat milk until very hot. (Do not boil.) Remove from heat and stir in honey and vanilla. Divide between four mugs and sprinkle with cinnamon.

Hot Christmas Punch

1½ quarts water
2 cups sugar
Juice of 3 oranges
Juice of 1 lemon
4 ounces red cinnamon candies
1 (20 ounce) can pineapple juice
2 quarts cranberry juice

In large saucepan, boil water, sugar, orange juice, lemon juice, and cinnamon candies. Stir and boil until candies are dissolved. Add in pineapple juice and cranberry juice and cook over medium heat, stirring until punch is thoroughly heated. Serve hot.

New Year's Eve Punch

1 (16 ounce) can fruit cocktail
2 (6 ounce) cans frozen orange juice concentrate
2 (6 ounce) cans frozen lemonade concentrate
2 (6 ounce) cans frozen limeade concentrate
2 (6 ounce) cans frozen pineapple concentrate
1 pint raspberry sherbet

Pour fruit cocktail into ring mold and freeze overnight.
Prepare frozen juices according to directions. Pour juices into
10-quart punch bowl and mix well. When ready to serve, float
fruit cocktail ring in punch. Scoop sherbet into center of fruit
cocktail ring.

Orange Eggnog Punch

1 quart eggnog
1 (12 ounce) can frozen orange juice concentrate, thawed
1 (12 ounce) can ginger ale, chilled

In pitcher, mix eggnog and orange juice concentrate until well blended. Gradually pour in ginger ale and stir gently.

And she shall bring forth a son, and thou shalt call his name Jesus: for he shall save his people from their sins.
MATTHEW 1:21 KJV

Orange Tea

7 cups water
1 (12 ounce) can frozen orange juice concentrate
½ cup sugar
2 tablespoons lemon juice
5 teaspoons instant tea mix
1 teaspoon whole cloves

In large saucepan, combine water, orange juice concentrate, sugar, lemon juice, and tea mix. Place cloves in tea ball or cheesecloth bag and add to saucepan. Simmer for 15 to 20 minutes. Remove cloves and serve hot.

·❦ Peppermint Christmas Punch ❦·

1 quart eggnog
½ (2 liter) bottle club soda
½ gallon vanilla ice cream, softened
Peppermint candies, crushed

Stir together eggnog, club soda, and ice cream. Blend well.
Sprinkle with crushed candies.

Spicy Orange-Apple Punch

1½ quarts orange juice
1 quart apple juice
⅓ cup light corn syrup

24 whole cloves
6 cinnamon sticks
12 thin lemon slices

Combine orange and apple juices, corn syrup, cloves, and cinnamon sticks in large saucepan. Gradually bring to boil. Reduce heat and simmer at least 5 to 10 minutes to blend flavors. Strain out cloves and cinnamon sticks. Serve hot with a lemon slice.

Experience an Inspiring Christmas at Home. . . .

A fun and simple idea for your Christmas dinner get-together: Tie a small ornament with ribbon around the napkins at each place setting. Your guests will appreciate these thoughtful little gifts.

Wassail

1 gallon apple cider
2 cups orange juice
1 (6 ounce) can frozen lemonade concentrate
2 teaspoons ground cinnamon
1 teaspoon ground nutmeg
1 teaspoon ground cloves
1 orange, cut into slices

Mix all ingredients except orange slices in large pan and slowly bring to boil. Simmer for 10 minutes. Float orange slices in hot wassail before serving.

Snowy Cinnamon Cocoa

4 cups milk
1 cup chocolate syrup
1 teaspoon ground cinnamon
Whipped topping
¼ cup semisweet chocolate chips

Place milk and chocolate syrup in a microwave-safe bowl and stir. Cook on high for 3 to 4 minutes or until hot. Stir in cinnamon. Pour into four large mugs and garnish with whipped topping and chocolate chips.

⋯⋰€ Pumpkin Nog 3⋱⋯

1 (29 ounce) can pumpkin puree
1 pint vanilla ice cream, softened
4 cups milk
1 teaspoon ground cinnamon
½ teaspoon ground nutmeg
¼ teaspoon ground ginger
1 cup whipped cream

Load a blender with small portions of pumpkin, ice cream, milk, and spices; blend thoroughly. Combine blended ingredients in large pitcher and pour into mugs. Top with whipped cream and a sprinkle of cinnamon if desired.

White Chocolate Coffee

3 ounces white chocolate, grated
2 cups whole milk
2 cups hot brewed coffee
Whipped topping, if desired

Place grated white chocolate and milk in microwave-safe bowl and heat for 2 minutes; stir until mixture is smooth and chocolate is melted completely. Stir in coffee. Serve in large mugs and top with whipped topping if desired.

World's Best Cocoa

¼ cup cocoa

½ cup sugar

⅓ cup hot water

⅛ teaspoon salt

4 cups milk

¾ teaspoon vanilla extract

Mix cocoa, sugar, water, and salt in saucepan. Over medium heat, stir constantly until mixture boils. Continue to stir and boil for 1 minute. Add milk and heat. (Do not boil.) Remove from heat and add vanilla; stir well. Pour into four mugs and serve immediately.

Hot Cranberry Punch

8 cups hot water
1½ cups sugar
¾ cup orange juice
¼ cup lemon juice
4 cups cranberry juice
12 whole cloves
½ cup red hot candies

In 5-quart slow cooker, combine water, sugar, and juices. Stir until sugar is dissolved. Place cloves in tea ball or cheesecloth, then place it and the candies in the slow cooker. Cover and cook on low for 2 to 3 hours until well heated. Remove cloves before serving.

Party Punch

5 cups double-strength tea, chilled
2¼ cups sugar
2½ cups orange juice
1½ cups unsweetened grapefruit juice
⅔ cup lemon juice
¼ cup lime juice
1½ quarts ginger ale, chilled

Combine all ingredients except for ginger ale. Cover punch and chill in refrigerator. When ready to serve, add chilled ginger ale. Stir to blend thoroughly.

Frothy Chocolate

3 cups milk
1 egg, beaten
⅓ cup semisweet chocolate chips
1 tablespoon sugar
½ teaspoon cinnamon
Whipped cream
Chocolate sprinkles

In medium saucepan, warm milk over medium-low heat until hot but not boiling. In small microwave-safe bowl, mix together egg, chocolate chips, sugar, and cinnamon. Microwave on high for 20-second intervals, stirring in between until melted and smooth. Add chocolate to milk and whisk together until well blended. Serve in mugs with whipped cream and chocolate sprinkles on top.

⋯⋅᷾᷈ Evergreen Punch ᷾᷈⋅⋯

1 (2 liter) bottle ginger ale
2 quarts water
1 (46 ounce) can pineapple juice
2 cups sugar
2 envelopes unsweetened lime drink mix

Combine all ingredients and mix well. Chill and serve.

Experience an Inspiring
Christmas at Home. ⋯

*Have a Christmas "picnic" with your family.
Even though it's blustery outside, you can still
enjoy this treat indoors. Spread a blanket on the
living room floor, pack simple foods in a picnic
basket (complete with holiday-themed napkins and
dinnerware), and feast in front of a blazing fire.
Top it off with marshmallows roasted over the fire.*

·····✤ Swedish Wassail ✤·····

1 gallon apple cider
1 pint water, boiled with
   6 small tea bags
1 quart pineapple juice
1 (12 ounce) can frozen
   orange juice
½ cup sugar

In cloth bag, combine:
2 cinnamon sticks
½ teaspoon whole cloves
1 teaspoon whole allspice

Combine first 5 ingredients in a large pot; add cloth bag ingredients. Simmer for 2 hours, uncovered. Serve hot.

Jesus did not come to make God's love possible, but to make God's love visible.
UNKNOWN

⋅⋅⋅❦ French Chocolate ❧⋅⋅⋅

½ cup semisweet chocolate pieces
½ cup white corn syrup
¼ cup water
1 teaspoon vanilla
1 pint whipping cream
2 quarts milk

In saucepan, blend chocolate, corn syrup, and water; heat over low heat until melted. Pour into cup and refrigerate until cool. Add vanilla. In large bowl, whip cream at medium speed, then gradually add chocolate mixture. Continue beating until mixture mounds. Spoon into punch bowl and chill. Scald milk, and pour into heated coffeepot. Spoon about 2 tablespoons of chocolate cream mixture into each cup and pour hot milk over chocolate. Stir.

Cranberry Tea

4 cups or 1 pound fresh cranberries
30 cloves
2½ quarts water, divided
2 scant cups sugar
1 cup orange juice

Cook cranberries and cloves in 2 quarts water until cranberries pop; strain. Save juice and discard cranberries and cloves. Dissolve sugar in 2 cups water and add to cranberry juice. Stir in orange juice. Serve hot.

Truffle Mugs

4 cups very hot, strong coffee
8 dark chocolate truffles, cut into quarters
Whipped cream for garnish

Pour coffee into 4 festive mugs and place truffle pieces in bowl.
Spoon whipped cream into serving dish. Serve coffee to your
guests and invite them to stir truffle pieces into their coffee.
Coffee should be stirred constantly until truffles have melted.
Guests can garnish their drinks with whipped cream if desired.

❈ Peppermint Iced Coffee ❈

Ice
¾ cup strong coffee
Peppermint coffee syrup
Skim milk or half-and-half

* * * ❈ ❈ ❈ ❈ ❈ * * *

Fill large glass with ice. In large mug, mix coffee and peppermint coffee syrup. Start with 1 teaspoon of syrup and add more to taste. Pour coffee mixture over ice and stir to start melting process. Add milk or half-and-half as desired.

Basic Hot Chocolate Mix

4 cups powdered chocolate milk mix
9½ cups powdered milk
1¾ cups powdered coffee creamer
1 cup powdered sugar

Mix all ingredients together and store in airtight container. Use ⅓ cup mix to 6-ounce mug of hot water. Serve with marshmallows.

And suddenly there was with the angel a multitude of the heavenly host praising God, and saying, Glory to God in the highest, and on earth, peace, good will toward men.
LUKE 2:13–14 KJV

Far East Spiced Tea

1 gallon boiling water
1 teaspoon cinnamon
3 cloves
3 small tea bags

1½ cups sugar
1 small can frozen
   orange juice
1 small can frozen lemon juice

In saucepan, combine water, cinnamon, cloves, and tea bags; boil for 2 minutes. Remove from heat. Add sugar; stir until dissolved. Strain, then add fruit juices. Bring to boil, stirring occasionally.

Experience an Inspiring Christmas at Home. . . .

Include the recipe for your "famous" dish with your Christmas cards this year. Print out several copies on Christmassy paper and add a personal note.

Mexican Hot Cocoa

3 cups water
1⅓ cups Basic Hot Chocolate Mix (see page 81)
½ teaspoon cinnamon
1 teaspoon vanilla
Whipped topping for garnish
4 cinnamon sticks for stirring

Combine water, hot chocolate mix, cinnamon, and vanilla in
blender. Mix on medium for 30 seconds or until well blended.
Pour into saucepan and heat until almost boiling. Pour into
4 mugs and garnish with a dollop of whipped cream and a
cinnamon stick.

Cranberry Spiced Cider

1 quart apple cider
2 cups cranberry juice cocktail
1 orange
1 lemon
½ teaspoon whole cloves
3 cinnamon sticks

Combine all ingredients in large stockpot and simmer on stove for about 1 hour. Ladle into cups and serve.

·‧·⊰ Sweet and Tangy Tea Mix ⊱‧·

2 cups orange drink mix
2 cups instant iced tea mix
2 cups sugar
¾ teaspoon cinnamon
¾ teaspoon ground cloves
1 teaspoon ginger
Thin orange slices for garnish

Mix all ingredients except orange slices in airtight container. Keep in cool, dry place. To serve, put 1 tablespoon mixture in mug and add hot water. Stir well and place slice of orange on side of cup.

Eggnog Punch

2 quarts french vanilla ice cream, divided
2 quarts Best Eggnog (see page 52), chilled
1 liter cream soda, chilled
Cinnamon
1 package large candy canes

Place ice cream in extra-large punch bowl. Add half eggnog. Stir and mash mixture using potato masher until ice cream is melted and mixture is well combined. Stir in remaining eggnog. Slowly pour in cream soda, stirring to combine. Sprinkle lightly with cinnamon. Hang candy canes around punch bowl for decoration and for guests to enjoy!

Spiced Apple Cider

2 quarts apple cider
1 large orange, cut into
    thin slices with peel
2 cinnamon sticks

¼ cup brown sugar
½ teaspoon salt
¼ teaspoon nutmeg
½ teaspoon ginger

In large saucepan, combine all ingredients and heat to almost boiling. Allow to cook for at least 30 minutes before serving. Serve with Christmas cookies.

Experience an Inspiring Christmas at Home. . . . .

A simple holiday tablecloth and special napkin rings are fuss-free ways to liven up your dining room for the holiday season.

⋯⋗ Apple Cider Nog ⋖⋯

3 cups milk
2 eggs
¼ cup sugar
1 cup apple cider
¼ teaspoon salt

¼ teaspoon cinnamon
Dash nutmeg
Whipped cream
Additional nutmeg

* * * * *

Heat milk in medium saucepan. Set aside. In bowl, beat eggs and sugar until light and fluffy. Add apple cider, salt, cinnamon, and nutmeg. Whisk egg mixture into hot milk. Heat, stirring constantly until mixture simmers. Do not boil. Pour immediately into mugs. Top with whipped cream and a dash of nutmeg.

Holiday Pineapple Punch

1 quart water
2 cups sugar
2 cups pineapple juice
Juice of 6 lemons
3 pints chilled ginger ale
Red and green maraschino cherries, if desired

Boil water and sugar for 20 minutes, then add pineapple and lemon juices. Stir and cool completely. Add ginger ale just before serving. As an added touch, freeze red and green maraschino cherries with water in ice cube trays, then add to punch.

·❧ Festive Pineapple-Grape Punch ❧·

1 cup sugar
2 cups water
1 pint grape juice
Juice of 2 oranges
Juice of 2 lemons
1 cup crushed pineapple
Crushed ice
Seedless grapes

* * * * *

Boil sugar and water for 1 minute. Chill, then add juices and pineapple. Pour into glasses partly filled with crushed ice and add a few seedless grapes.

Merry
Main Dishes

*Christmas is the season
for kindling the fire of hospitality
in the hall, the genial flame
of charity in the heart.*
WASHINGTON IRVING

⋯❧ Ham with Coke ❧⋯

1 ham
Cloves
1 small can pineapple rings
Brown sugar
Water
1 (12 ounce) can Coke, divided

* * * * *

Place ham in roaster. Stud with cloves. Put pineapple rings on ham with toothpicks. Put brown sugar in holes of pineapple. Pour water over brown sugar to moisten. Bake at 325 degrees for 1 hour. Baste with half can of Coke. Bake another hour and baste with remaining Coke. Continue baking until done.

Veal in Wine with Mushrooms

3 pounds veal, cut into 1-inch cubes
2 tablespoons butter
2 (4½ ounce) cans mushroom caps
½ cup cooking oil
1 cup white cooking wine
½ cup onions, chopped
1 teaspoon oregano
1 cup sour cream
5⅓ cups cooked rice

Brown veal in butter. Add remaining ingredients except sour cream and rice; simmer 30 to 40 minutes until tender. Remove from heat and add sour cream; serve with cooked rice.

Flank Steak Marinade

½ cup soy sauce
¼ cup brown sugar
1 clove garlic, minced, or ½ teaspoon garlic powder
2 tablespoons vegetable oil
1 teaspoon ground ginger
½ teaspoon monosodium glutamate
Flank steak (approximately 2 pounds)

For marinade, combine all ingredients except steak. Mix well. Score both sides of steak and place in glass 9x13-inch baking dish. Spoon marinade over steak and let stand for at least 2 hours at room temperature, turning steak over about every 30 minutes. (Steak can be marinated in the refrigerator but will require approximately 4 hours to achieve the same degree of flavor as at room temperature.) Remove from marinade and broil steak under broiler or grill over coals. Slice steak across grain and serve. Marinade is also good with chicken, pork chops, or ribs.

Oriental Charcoal Broiled Roast

5 ounces soy sauce
2 cups tomato juice
Juice of 2 lemons

1 tablespoon dehydrated
    onion
2 to 3 pounds chuck roast,
    cut about 2 inches thick

Combine soy sauce, tomato juice, lemon juice, and onion to make marinade. Marinate roast for several hours or overnight. Grill over hot charcoals; cut into thin slices to serve.

Experience an Inspiring Christmas at Home. . . .

A great way to warm hearts on cold winter days is to tell your loved ones how much they mean to you. That, along with a steaming mug of hot chocolate, can't be beat!

Shrimp Newburg

6 tablespoons butter
2 tablespoons flour
1½ cups light cream
3 egg yolks, beaten
2 cups cooked shrimp
2 teaspoons lemon juice
3 tablespoons water or chicken broth
¼ teaspoon salt
Paprika to taste
Toast points

In saucepan, blend butter and flour; add cream all at once. Heat over low heat and stir until thickened. Stir small amount of hot mixture into yolks and return to the pan. Cook, stirring until thick. Add shrimp, then add lemon juice, water or broth, salt, and paprika. Serve with toast points.

Garlic and Rosemary
Leg of Lamb

Leg of lamb
Garlic cloves
Salt and pepper
Flour
Dried rosemary
Water

Ask your butcher to bone and tie leg. Push garlic cloves into inside of lamb. Rub salt, pepper, and flour all over lamb. Place in roasting pan and sprinkle with dried rosemary. Cook at 350 degrees for 30 minutes per pound of meat. Add water to pan as needed. Remove lamb and make gravy with drippings.

Chicken Orange

1 chicken, cut into pieces
Herbs as desired
½ cup butter, melted
1 small can frozen orange juice concentrate

Remove skin from chicken and arrange pieces in baking dish. Sprinkle with herbs. Combine melted butter and undiluted orange juice. Pour mixture over chicken and bake at 350 degrees, uncovered, for 1 hour.

"Glory to God in the highest heaven, and on earth peace to those on whom his favor rests."
LUKE 2:14 NIV

Baked Pork Chops and Apples

4 to 6 apples, peeled
    and sliced
½ cup brown sugar
2 tablespoons flour
½ teaspoon cinnamon
¼ teaspoon nutmeg
6 pork chops, browned

Mix apples, sugar, flour, and spices; place in oblong baking dish. Top with browned pork chops. Cover and bake 1½ hours at 375 degrees. Serve with apples and sauce on top of pork chops.

···❊ Huntington Chicken ❊···

4 cups chicken broth
8 tablespoons flour
½ pound processed cheese, grated
1 (4 to 5 pound) whole chicken, stewed and boned
2 cups macaroni (measured after cooking)
Salt and pepper to taste
7 slices bread, crumbled
¼ cup butter, melted

* * * * * ❊ ❊ ❊ ❊ ❊ * * * *

In a large saucepan, heat broth. Take a cup of broth and blend with flour to make a paste. Add to pan of broth to create gravy. Stir in cheese until melted. Add chicken and macaroni. Place in ungreased 9x13-inch baking dish. Combine bread with butter and spread over top of casserole. Bake at 350 degrees for 45 minutes, or until bubbly. (Casserole may be frozen without topping prior to baking.)

Lamb Stew

1 pound lamb, cut into
  ¾-inch pieces
2 tablespoons olive oil
3 cups beef broth
3 cloves garlic, minced
1 teaspoon ground marjoram
1 bay leaf
¼ teaspoon salt

¼ teaspoon black pepper
2 large potatoes, peeled and
  cut into ½-inch chunks
1½ cups carrots, sliced
1½ cups celery, chopped
½ cup onion, chopped
½ cup sour cream
3 tablespoons flour

In large soup pot, brown meat in oil; drain excess fat. Add broth, garlic, marjoram, bay leaf, salt, and pepper and bring to a boil. Reduce heat, cover, and simmer for 20 minutes until meat is rather tender. Add potatoes, carrots, celery, and onion. Bring to a boil again and then reduce heat, cover, and simmer for 30 minutes until vegetables are tender. Remove bay leaf. In a bowl, blend sour cream and flour, then stir in ½ cup of liquid from stew. Add sour cream mixture to stew and cook until thickened.

Home-Style Turkey

1 (12 to 14 pound) whole turkey
6 tablespoons butter, divided
3 tablespoons chicken bouillon
4 cups warm water
2 tablespoons dried minced onion
2 tablespoons dried parsley
2 tablespoons seasoning salt

Rinse turkey and remove giblet packet from inside. Put turkey on rack in roasting pan. Cut approximately 6 pockets into skin over each breast and insert approximately 1 tablespoon butter in each pocket. In bowl, dissolve bouillon in water; add onion and parsley. Pour over turkey. Sprinkle seasoning salt all over turkey. Cover turkey with foil and bake at 350 degrees for 3 hours; remove foil. Bake another 30 to 60 minutes. Insert thermometer to check that meat has reached 180 degrees. Remove and let rest 15 minutes before carving.

Venison Roast

1 (3 to 5 pound) venison roast
¼ teaspoon pepper
¼ teaspoon salt
¼ cup oil
2 cans cream of mushroom soup
1 envelope dry onion soup mix
1½ cups water
1 (6.5 ounce) can mushrooms, drained
2 cloves garlic, minced

Sprinkle meat with pepper and salt. In skillet, brown all sides of roast in oil. Combine soups and water; add mushrooms and garlic; pour over roast. Set slow cooker temperature on low and cook approximately 6 hours or until meat easily pulls apart. Or bake in a dutch oven at 375 degrees for 3 to 4 hours.

Pheasant with Wild Rice Stuffing

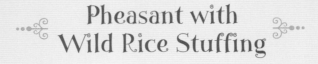

3 pounds cleaned pheasant
2 tablespoons butter
¾ cup celery, diced
¼ cup onion, diced
1 cup mushrooms,
   thinly sliced

1 teaspoon salt
¼ teaspoon pepper
1 tablespoon dried parsley
½ teaspoon dried rosemary
1½ cups cooked wild rice
3 bacon slices

Rinse pheasant; pat dry. Melt butter in frying pan. Add celery, onion, and mushrooms. Sauté until vegetables are tender and translucent. Remove from heat. Add remaining ingredients, except bacon, tossing with fork. Spoon stuffing into cavity of bird and truss by tying a piece of string to end of neck skin and pulling it over back. Slip ends of wings over back and press them close to body. Press thighs close to body and draw ends of string back on each side and up over thighs. Cross string between legs and tie down under the tail. Place bird on rack in shallow roasting pan. Lay bacon slices over top breast. Roast at 325 degrees for 2 hours, basting occasionally with pan drippings. Remove string before cutting and serving.

Lasagna

1 pound Italian sausage
1 clove garlic,
    minced
1 tablespoon whole basil
1½ teaspoons salt
1 (1 pound) can tomatoes
2 (6 ounce) cans tomato
    paste
10 ounces lasagna noodles
2 eggs

3 cups fresh ricotta or cream-
    style cottage cheese
½ cup grated Parmesan
    or romano cheese
2 tablespoons parsley flakes
1 teaspoon salt
½ teaspoon pepper
1 pound mozzarella cheese,
    sliced very thin

Brown sausage slowly and spoon off excess fat. Add next 5 ingredients plus 1 cup of water and simmer covered for 15 minutes; stir frequently. Cook noodles in boiling salted water until tender. Beat eggs and add remaining ingredients except mozzarella. Layer half lasagna noodles in 13x9x2-inch baking dish; spread with half of ricotta filling; then half of mozzarella cheese and half of meat sauce. Repeat. Bake at 375 degrees for 30 minutes.

···❦ Honey Roast Ham ❧···

4½ pound cured ham, leg or
    shoulder roast
1 onion
Cloves
2 bay leaves
A few black peppercorns
Few stalks of parsley
Twist of orange peel

Small piece of fresh ginger
½ cinnamon stick

GLAZE
2 tablespoons whole
    grain mustard
6 tablespoons clear
    honey

* * * * ❄ ❄ ❄ ❄ * * * *

Calculate cooking time for ham, figuring 20 minutes per
pound, adding an extra 20 minutes. In order to draw off salt
used in curing process, place ham in large pan and cover with
cold water. Bring to boil and remove from heat. Pour off water
and replace with cold water, adding onion, cloves, and other
flavoring ingredients. Bring to boil slowly; cover and simmer
for calculated time, subtracting 15 minutes. Remove ham from
pan and cool slightly. Heat oven to 350 degrees. Score fat of
ham in diamond pattern with sharp knife and press cloves into
fat at intervals. Combine honey and mustard and spread over
skin. Wrap ham in foil, leaving glazed area uncovered. Bake in
roasting pan for 15 minutes. Serve hot or cold.

Herbed Salmon Steaks

2 tablespoons margarine
   or butter
2 tablespoons lemon
   juice
4 salmon steaks,
   ¾-inch thick

1 teaspoon onion salt
¼ teaspoon pepper
½ teaspoon dried marjoram
   or thyme leaves
Paprika
Lemon wedges

Place margarine and lemon juice in a 12x7½x2-inch baking dish and heat in a 400-degree oven. Coat both sides of fish with lemon butter and place in baking dish. Sprinkle with seasonings and bake uncovered about 25 minutes, or until fish flakes easily with fork. Sprinkle with paprika and serve with lemon wedges and parsley.

*Dear heavenly Father, I admit I'm feeling a little less than cheerful this Christmas. I have so much I need to accomplish that I'm losing my passion and excitement for the holiday celebrations. Please help me keep my focus on the things that matter most—and to forget about the things that aren't important. Restore the joy of Christmas to my heart.
Thank You, Lord. Amen.*

Savory Pork Roast

4 pound pork boneless top loin roast
1 clove garlic, cut into halves
1 teaspoon salt
1 teaspoon dried sage leaves
1 teaspoon dried marjoram leaves

Rub pork roast using cut sides of garlic. After mixing remaining ingredients, sprinkle on roast and place fat side up in shallow roasting pan. Insert meat thermometer in thickest part of pork and roast uncovered in a 325-degree oven for 2 to 2½ hours, or until meat thermometer registers 170 degrees. Garnish with frosted grapes (dipped in water and rolled in sugar) if desired.

Roast Goose with Browned Potatoes

1 goose (9 to 11 pounds)
Salt and pepper
4 to 6 large potatoes, pared and cut into halves
Paprika

Remove excess fat from goose. Lightly rub salt into cavity of goose. With skewer, fasten neck skin to back. Fold wings across back with tips touching and tie drumsticks to tail. Pierce skin liberally with fork. Place goose in shallow roasting pan breast side up and roast uncovered in a 350-degree oven for 3 to 3½ hours, removing excess fat from pan occasionally. One hour and 15 minutes before goose is done, place potatoes around goose in roasting pan. Brush potatoes with goose drippings and sprinkle with salt, pepper, and paprika. Place tent of aluminum foil loosely over goose to prevent excessive browning if necessary. After baking, cover and let stand 15 minutes for easier carving.

Herbed Cornish Hens

3 Rock Cornish hens (about 1
    pound each), thawed
Salt and pepper
¼ cup margarine or
    butter, melted

½ teaspoon dried
    marjoram leaves
½ teaspoon dried
    thyme leaves
¼ teaspoon paprika

Rub cavities of hens with salt and pepper. Combine margarine, marjoram, thyme, and paprika; brush portion of mixture on hens that have been placed in shallow baking pan, breast side up. Roast uncovered in 350-degree oven, brushing with remaining margarine mixture 5 or 6 times until done (about 1 hour). Cut each hen into halves with scissors, cutting along backbone from tail to neck and down center of breast. Garnish with watercress.

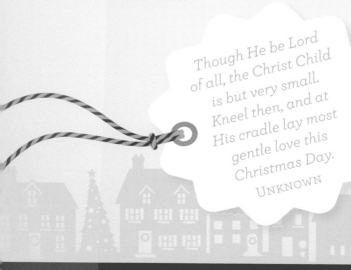

Though He be Lord of all, the Christ Child is but very small. Kneel then, and at His cradle lay most gentle love this Christmas Day.

UNKNOWN

Beef Burgundy

2 tablespoons olive oil
1½ to 2 pounds cubed
   stew meat
½ cup chopped onion
1 (10 ounce) can condensed
   cream of mushroom soup

¼ cup red wine vinegar
¼ cup reduced-salt beef broth
¼ teaspoon garlic powder
1 cup sliced fresh mushrooms
Egg noodles or rice, prepared

Heat oil in skillet. Add stew meat and brown. Remove meat from heat. Add onions to pan and sauté until tender. In ovenproof casserole, mix meat, onion, soup, vinegar, broth, and garlic powder. Bake, covered, at 325 degrees for 3 hours. The last 20 minutes, add mushrooms and return casserole to oven. Serve over egg noodles or rice.

·⊰ Broiled Shrimp ⊱·

1 cup butter
2 garlic cloves, minced
¼ cup lemon juice
½ teaspoon salt
¼ teaspoon freshly ground black pepper
2 pounds large shrimp, peeled and deveined
Chopped fresh parsley

In saucepan over low heat, melt butter with garlic, but don't allow garlic to scorch. Remove from heat and add lemon juice, salt, and pepper. Place shrimp in shallow baking dish and pour sauce over shrimp. Broil shrimp 4 to 5 inches from heating element for 6 to 8 minutes. Turn and baste shrimp halfway through. When done, shrimp should be pink and tender. Garnish with chopped fresh parsley.

Chicken Diane

4 large boneless chicken
  breast halves
½ teaspoon salt
½ teaspoon black pepper
2 tablespoons olive
  oil, divided
2 tablespoons butter or
  margarine, divided

3 tablespoons chopped
  fresh chives
Juice of ½ lemon
3 tablespoons chopped
  fresh parsley
2 teaspoons Dijon mustard
¼ cup chicken broth

Place each chicken breast between two sheets of waxed paper
and pound to flatten slightly. Sprinkle chicken with salt and
pepper. Set aside. In large skillet, heat 1 tablespoon each of oil
and butter. Cook each chicken breast in skillet for 4 minutes on
each side. Transfer to warm serving platter. Add chives, lemon
juice, parsley, and mustard to skillet. Cook for 15 seconds,
whisking constantly. Whisk in the broth and stir until sauce
is smooth. Whisk in remaining oil and butter. Pour sauce over
chicken and serve immediately.

Cornish Hens with Basil-Walnut Sauce

1 bunch fresh basil
½ cup grated Parmesan
   cheese
1 clove garlic
Salt and pepper to taste
¼ cup walnuts

2 Cornish game hens,
   split and quartered
Butter
½ cup chicken stock
½ cup heavy cream
Additional basil and
   walnuts for garnish

In food processor basket, combine first five ingredients. Puree to smooth paste. Set aside. In large skillet, cook hens in butter until tender. Transfer to warm platter. Drain grease from skillet and pour in chicken stock. Cook until stock is reduced by half. Add cream and again reduce to half. Stir in 2 tablespoons of basil-walnut paste. Add additional salt and pepper if needed. Pour sauce over hens and garnish with basil and walnuts.

Glazed Ham

1 (7 to 10 pound) fully
   cooked ham
1 (2 liter) bottle Dr Pepper

1 tablespoon ground cloves
1 teaspoon ground cinnamon
Whole cloves

Place ham in roasting pan and cover with mixture of Dr Pepper and spices. Bake ham at 325 degrees for 1½ hours. Remove from oven and score top of ham. Stud ham with cloves.

Mix together:
1 teaspoon ground cinnamon
1 teaspoon dry mustard
Dr Pepper

Add enough Dr Pepper to form paste. Brush mixture over scored ham.

Mix together:
1 cup brown sugar
¼ cup Dr Pepper, or enough to form a paste

Brush final mixture over ham. Bake an additional 1½ hours or until ham reaches an internal temperature of 140 degrees.

Home-Style Roast Beef

1 (10 to 12 pound) bottom
round beef roast
1 (14½ ounce) can
chicken broth
1 (10¼ ounce) can beef gravy
1 (10¾ ounce) can condensed
cream of celery soup
¼ cup water
¼ cup Worcestershire sauce

¼ cup soy sauce
3 tablespoons dried
parsley flakes
3 tablespoons dill weed
2 tablespoons dried thyme
4½ teaspoons garlic powder
1 teaspoon celery salt
1 teaspoon black pepper
1 large onion, sliced into rings

Place roast in large roasting pan, fat side up. Prick meat
with meat fork. In bowl, combine broth, gravy, soup, water,
Worcestershire, and soy sauce. Pour mixture evenly over roast,
then sprinkle with seasonings. Place onion rings over roast.
Bake, uncovered, at 325 degrees for 2½ to 3½ hours or until
meat reaches desired doneness. Meat thermometer should read
140 degrees for a rare roast, 160 degrees for a medium roast,
and 170 degrees for a well-done roast. Let stand for 15 to 20
minutes before slicing.

⋅⋅❧ Lemon-Herb Turkey Breast ⦂⋅⋅

1 (8 to 9 pound) bone-in
   turkey breast
3 tablespoons fresh
   lemon juice, divided
2 tablespoons olive
   oil, divided
2 garlic cloves, crushed
1¼ teaspoons salt

1 teaspoon grated lemon peel
1 teaspoon dried thyme
1 teaspoon freshly ground
   black pepper
½ teaspoon ground sage
Lemon-pepper
   seasoning to taste

Rinse turkey in cold water and pat dry. Loosen skin from turkey with fingers, but leave skin attached to meat. In small bowl, combine 1 tablespoon lemon juice, 1 tablespoon oil, garlic, salt, lemon peel, thyme, pepper, and sage. Spread evenly under turkey skin. Combine remaining lemon juice and oil; set aside. Place turkey on rack in shallow roasting pan sprayed with cooking spray. Bake uncovered at 350 degrees for 2½ to 3 hours or until meat thermometer reads 170 degrees, basting every 15 to 20 minutes with lemon juice and oil mixture. Let stand for 10 to 15 minutes before carving.

Orange Duck

½ cup orange juice
½ cup apple jelly
1 dash pepper
1 (5 pound) dressed duck
Salt and pepper to taste
1 large stalk celery, cut
    into 2-inch pieces

1 small onion, quartered
⅔ cup long-grain
    rice, uncooked
1 (12¾ ounce) package
    instant wild rice
⅓ cup chopped fresh parsley

Combine orange juice, jelly, and pepper in small saucepan. Cook over medium heat until jelly melts and mixture bubbles, stirring frequently. Remove from heat and keep warm. Rub cavity of duck with salt and pepper; place celery and onion pieces in cavity. Place duck, breast side up, on a rack in a roasting pan. Baste lightly with melted jelly mixture. Bake, uncovered at 375 degrees for 1 hour, basting frequently with jelly mixture. If duck starts to brown too much, cover loosely with aluminum foil. Bake for an additional 1 to 1½ hours or until meat thermometer registers 185 degrees when placed in thickest part of duck breast, basting frequently. Prepare long-grain rice and wild rice according to package directions. Combine cooked rice and parsley; stir well. Spoon onto serving platter. Place duck on top of rice.

Oven-Fried Chicken

¼ cup butter or margarine, melted and divided

⅓ cup cornmeal

⅓ cup flour

¼ teaspoon paprika

¼ teaspoon salt

¼ teaspoon garlic powder

2 tablespoons grated Parmesan cheese

4 to 6 boneless, skinless chicken breasts

Pour half of butter in long baking dish and set aside. Combine next six ingredients in sealed plastic bag. Shake each piece of chicken in mixture to coat. Place chicken pieces in baking dish, and pour remaining butter over chicken. Bake at 350 degrees for 1 hour and 15 minutes.

Experience an Inspiring Christmas at Home. · · · ·

Decorate three-ring binders to create family cookbooks. Include recipes for all your family favorites with a brief bio and photo of the creator of each dish. These gifts will be cherished for years to come.

Rotisserie-Style Chicken

1 (4 to 5 pound) whole chicken
2 teaspoons salt
1 teaspoon paprika
½ teaspoon onion powder
½ teaspoon ground thyme

½ teaspoon black pepper
½ teaspoon dried oregano
¼ teaspoon cayenne pepper
¼ teaspoon garlic powder
1 onion, quartered

Remove giblets from chicken. Rinse out chicken cavity and pat chicken dry. Set aside. In small bowl, mix together spices. Rub spice mixture on inside and outside of chicken. Place onion inside chicken cavity. Place chicken in sealable bag and refrigerate overnight. Remove chicken from bag and place in roasting pan. Bake uncovered at 250 degrees for 5 hours or until internal temperature reaches 180 degrees.

❧ Italian Turkey ❧

1½ pounds ground salt pork
1 garlic clove, minced
3 teaspoons ground sage

2½ to 3⅓ teaspoons
   chili powder
Salt and pepper to taste
1 (10 to 12 pound) turkey

Combine first five ingredients and spread over turkey. Bake at 350 degrees for 4½ hours or until done. Remove pork mixture from turkey and place in large bowl; crumble mixture with fork. Debone turkey and chop meat into small pieces. Blend turkey with pork mixture. Serve as loose meat or with rolls for sandwiches.

The Son
is the image of the
invisible God,
the firstborn over
all creation.
COLOSSIANS 1:15 NIV

Shrimp with Pasta

16 ounces vermicelli
Salt and pepper to taste
½ cup butter
½ cup olive oil
4 cloves garlic, minced
24 large shrimp, peeled
   and deveined

8 large fresh mushrooms,
   sliced
1 cup chopped fresh parsley
Romano cheese

Cook vermicelli in boiling water for 10 minutes. Drain and rinse in cold water. Toss noodles with salt and pepper and set aside. In large skillet, heat butter and oil. Add garlic, shrimp, and mushrooms. Cook until shrimp turns pink, about 5 minutes. Toss in vermicelli and heat through. Transfer to warmed platter and sprinkle with parsley and cheese.

Sweet-and-Sour Chops

4 loin-cut pork chops,
   excess fat trimmed
4 medium potatoes, cut
   into ¾-inch slices
2 (10 ounce) cans condensed
   cream of mushroom soup
1 small onion, diced
1 clove garlic, minced
3 tablespoons honey
3 tablespoons prepared
   mustard

3 tablespoons lemon juice
½ teaspoon Worcestershire
   sauce
½ teaspoon dried
   parsley flakes
½ teaspoon ground sage
½ teaspoon ground thyme
Salt and pepper to taste

In large skillet, quickly brown pork chops on both sides. Place pork chops in large baking dish and set aside. Boil potatoes in salted water until slightly softened. Drain well and layer over pork chops. In large bowl, combine remaining ingredients; stir until thoroughly combined. Pour mixture over potatoes and chops. Bake at 350 degrees for 25 to 30 minutes or until pork chops are done.

Traditional Christmas Turkey

1 (10 to 12 pound)
    whole turkey
6 tablespoons butter,
    cut into slices
3 cubes chicken bouillon
4 cups warm water

2 tablespoons dried
    parsley flakes
2 tablespoons minced onion
2 tablespoons seasoned salt
2 tablespoons poultry
    seasoning

Rinse turkey. Remove neck and discard giblets. Place turkey in roasting pan. Separate skin over breast and place slices of butter between skin and breast meat. In small bowl, dissolve bouillon in water. Stir in parsley and minced onion and pour mixture over top of turkey. Sprinkle turkey with seasoned salt and poultry seasoning. Cover with foil and bake at 350 degrees for 3½ to 4 hours, until internal temperature of turkey reaches 180 degrees. Remove foil during last 45 minutes to brown turkey.

Turkey Scaloppini

½ to ¾ pound turkey cutlets
½ cup flour
½ teaspoon salt
¼ teaspoon black pepper
¼ teaspoon dried basil
3 tablespoons butter or
   margarine, divided
2 tablespoons olive oil

1 clove garlic, minced
¼ pound sliced fresh
   mushrooms
2 tablespoons lemon juice
⅓ cup chicken broth
¼ cup white wine or
   additional chicken broth

Between sheets of waxed paper, pound cutlets to ⅛-inch thickness. Combine flour, salt, pepper, and basil. Dredge cutlets in seasoned flour and shake off excess. In skillet, melt 2 tablespoons butter. Add oil and stir in garlic. Brown each cutlet until golden, approximately 3 minutes. Place browned meat in ovenproof casserole dish. Melt remaining tablespoon of butter in skillet; add mushrooms. Sauté until mushrooms have softened; spoon over meat. In same skillet, combine lemon juice with broth and wine. Cook until heated through. Pour over casserole. Bake at 325 degrees for 30 to 35 minutes.

Country Holiday Ham

1 (7 pound) sugar-cured ham
Whole cloves
2 cups maple pancake syrup
½ cup cola

Preheat oven to 350 degrees. Remove skin from ham. Score fat surface of ham with knife in diamond shape or any design, and stud with cloves. Pour syrup then cola over ham. Cover with foil and bake for 3 to 4 hours, checking after 3 hours to make sure ham isn't getting dry.

Experience an Inspiring Christmas at Home. · · · ·

Looking for a simple but pretty holiday centerpiece for your dining room table? Fill a glass bowl with snowflake- or other holiday-shaped confetti along with some candy canes. Colored bulb ornaments make for a festive centerpiece, too.

Holiday Ham Casserole

3 tablespoons butter
2 cups ham, cooked and cubed
1 (8.5 ounce) can pineapple
  chunks, drained
1 (10.5 ounce) can onion
  soup

3 tablespoons brown sugar
Salt and pepper to taste
1 (10.5 ounce) can sweet
  potatoes, drained
½ cup chopped walnuts

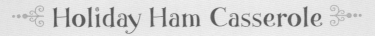

In large saucepan, heat butter and ham until lightly browned.
Add pineapple chunks, onion soup, and 1 tablespoon brown
sugar. Season with salt and pepper to taste. Bring to boil, then
remove from heat. Spoon into buttered casserole dish. Place
sweet potato slices in an even layer over ham and pineapple
mixture. Combine walnuts and remaining brown sugar. Spread
over sweet potatoes. Bake for 30 minutes in a 400-degree oven.

Roast Beef with Yorkshire Pudding

1 (4 to 6) pound boneless rib roast
Salt and pepper to taste
1 recipe Yorkshire Pudding Batter (see page 129)

Place rib roast on rack in shallow roasting pan with fat side up. Sprinkle with salt and pepper and insert meat thermometer in thickest part of beef, avoiding fat. Roast in 325-degree oven uncovered for about 1¾ hours or to desired degree of doneness: 130 to 135 degrees for rare, and 150 to 155 degrees for medium. Shortly before beef is done, prepare Yorkshire Pudding Batter (see next page for recipe). Remove beef from oven and transfer to platter; cover with aluminum foil. Heat 9x9x2-inch baking pan in oven at 425 degrees. Reserve ¼ cup meat drippings, adding vegetable oil if necessary, and pour into heated pan. Add pudding batter and bake 25 minutes or until puffed and golden brown. Cut into squares and serve with sliced roast beef.

Yorkshire Pudding Batter

1 cup all-purpose flour
1 cup milk
2 eggs
½ teaspoon salt

Beat all ingredients until smooth.

Once in royal David's city
Stood a lowly cattle shed,
Where a mother laid her baby
In a manger for His bed:
Mary was that mother mild,
Jesus Christ, her little child.
CECIL FRANCES ALEXANDER

Festive Holiday Ham

1 (7 pound) smoked ham
2 cups water
Olive oil
Whole cloves to cover ham
1 cup brown sugar
2 tablespoons flour
⅛ teaspoon garlic powder

⅛ teaspoon onion powder
⅛ teaspoon black pepper
1 (16 ounce) can sliced
   pineapple rings
1 jar maraschino cherries,
   cut into halves

Place ham in roaster with water. Cover and bake at 325 degrees for 3½ to 4½ hours. If ham has exposed bone, cover with foil. Spray ham occasionally with olive oil during first part of cooking. Continue roasting until a thermometer inserted in center reads 160 degrees. Be sure thermometer is not touching bone. When ham is done, remove from oven. Lift off rind. Using sharp knife, score fat surface crosswise, and dot with cloves. Set aside. Combine brown sugar and flour. Rub mixture over scored ham. Sprinkle lightly with garlic powder, onion powder, and black pepper. Place pineapple slices on ham with cloves in center. Cover cloves with maraschino cherry half. Continue until ham is covered decoratively with pineapple slices and cherries. Brown uncovered for 20 minutes in a 400-degree oven.

Bierock Casserole

2 pounds lean ground beef
1 medium onion, diced
1 small head cabbage,
   chopped

Salt and pepper to taste
1 (36 count) package
   frozen rolls

In large skillet, brown meat with diced onion. Add cabbage; cover and cook until cabbage is tender. Add salt and pepper to taste. Grease two 9x13-inch baking pans. Place 18 rolls in each pan. Let rise. Press down gently. Spoon cabbage mixture on top of rolls in one pan. Flip rolls from other pan over top of cabbage. Press down lightly. Bake at 350 degrees for 30 to 35 minutes or until rolls are browned.

Experience an Inspiring Christmas at Home....

This Christmas, clear your mind of all the clutter. Forget about having a spotless house. Forget about shopping. Forget about having the perfect decorations. Forget about planning the perfect holiday menu. Instead, take time to reflect on God's Gift of Hope He sent on that silent night so long ago.

Creamy Chicken and Rice with Thyme

¾ cup chicken broth or water
½ teaspoon salt
1½ cups quick-cooking rice
1½ to 2 pounds split chicken breast
1 (6 ounce) can sliced mushrooms with liquid
1 (10.5 ounce) can cream of mushroom soup
½ teaspoon thyme
1 tablespoon fine bread crumbs
1 tablespoon melted butter

* * * * * ✳ ✳ ✳ ✳ ✳ * * * *

In greased pan, combine first 3 ingredients. Place chicken over rice mixture. Combine mushrooms and soup. Spread over chicken. Sprinkle with thyme, bread crumbs, and butter. Cover tightly with foil and bake at 400 degrees for 1 hour, or until chicken is done.

Ham with Apple Relish

1 teaspoon ground cloves
1 (3 to 4 pound) fully
   cooked boneless ham
4 medium tart apples,
   peeled and chopped
2 cups sugar
1 cup chopped dried apricots

½ cup dried cranberries
½ cup golden raisins
¼ cup white vinegar
2 tablespoons grated
   orange peel
½ teaspoon ground ginger

Rub cloves over ham. Wrap ham tightly in foil and bake at 325 degrees for 1 to 1½ hours or until internal temperature reaches 140 degrees. Meanwhile, combine remaining ingredients in a saucepan for relish. Stirring constantly, bring mixture to boil. Reduce heat and simmer for 25 to 30 minutes or until thickened. Serve relish over ham slices.

Seasonal Sides & Salads

*Blessed is the season
which engages the
whole world in a
conspiracy of love.*
HAMILTON WRIGHT MABIE

Corn Bread Dressing

4 stalks celery, diced
2 medium onions, diced
¼ cup butter or
    margarine, melted
6 cups prepared crumbled
    corn bread
5 slices day-old bread, wheat
    or white, crumbled
1 pound bulk pork sausage,
    cooked and drained

1½ cups finely chopped
    cooked ham
¾ cup almonds, toasted
    and chopped
¾ cup chopped fresh parsley
1½ teaspoons black pepper
1 teaspoon poultry seasoning
1 teaspoon ground sage
2 cups chicken broth
1 egg, lightly beaten

Sauté celery and onion in butter until tender. Combine with breads, sausage, ham, almonds, and seasonings in a large bowl; toss well. Add broth and egg to corn bread mixture; stir well. If desired, dressing may be baked separately from turkey in lightly greased 9x13-inch baking dish. Bake uncovered at 350 degrees for 45 minutes to 1 hour or until lightly browned. Unstuffed turkey should be baked 5 minutes less per pound than stuffed turkey.

Almond Rice

1¾ cups water
½ cup orange juice
½ teaspoon salt
1 cup uncooked long-
    grain rice
2 tablespoons butter
    or margarine
2 tablespoons brown sugar

½ cup sliced natural almonds
1 teaspoon minced
    crystallized ginger
¼ teaspoon grated
    orange peel
Additional orange
    peel, if desired

In medium saucepan, bring water, orange juice, and salt to boil; gradually add rice, stirring constantly. Cover, reduce heat, and simmer for 20 to 25 minutes or until rice is tender and liquid is absorbed. Meanwhile, melt butter and brown sugar in small skillet over medium heat. Stir in almonds and ginger; sauté for 2 minutes or until almonds are lightly browned. Add almond mixture and grated orange peel to rice; stir gently to combine. Garnish with additional orange peel if desired.

Farmhouse Potato Salad

4 cups hash browns
1 tablespoon salt in 1 quart boiling water
¼ cup sour cream
1 teaspoon salt
¼ teaspoon pepper
4 tablespoons diced sweet pickles
½ teaspoon mustard
¼ cup chopped celery
2 tablespoons sweet onions, chopped
2 hard-boiled eggs, shelled and chopped

Cook hash browns and 1 tablespoon salt in water in large covered saucepan until tender. Drain. Set aside. Combine sour cream, salt, pepper, pickles, and mustard. Mix until smooth. Add celery, onions, and eggs. Stir lightly. Pour over warm potatoes. Toss lightly and cover. Refrigerate for several hours. Serve chilled.

·⁂ Chive Mashed Potatoes ⁂·

2½ pounds potatoes, about 8 medium,
    peeled and cut into 1-inch cubes
1 (8 ounce) package cream cheese, cubed and softened
¾ to 1 cup milk
½ cup snipped fresh chives
1¼ teaspoons salt
¼ teaspoon black pepper

Boil potatoes in covered medium saucepan in 2 inches water
for 10 to 12 minutes or until tender; drain. Return to pan and
mash with electric mixer or potato masher, gradually stirring
in cream cheese until blended. Blend in milk, chives, salt, and
pepper. Stir gently over medium heat until heated through.
Serve immediately.

Creamy Corn Casserole

3 tablespoons butter or margarine, divided
1 cup finely chopped celery
¼ cup finely chopped onion
¼ cup finely chopped red pepper
1 (10¾ ounce) can condensed cream of chicken soup
3 cups fresh, frozen, or canned corn, drained
1 (8 ounce) can sliced water chestnuts, drained
½ cup soft bread crumbs

Melt 2 tablespoons butter in medium skillet. Add celery, onion, and red pepper and sauté until vegetables are tender, about 2 minutes. Remove from heat and stir in soup, corn, and water chestnuts. Spoon into greased 2-quart casserole dish. Toss bread crumbs with remaining 1 tablespoon melted butter. Sprinkle on top of casserole and bake uncovered at 350 degrees for 25 to 30 minutes.

English Pea Casserole

½ cup chopped onion
1 small sweet red pepper, chopped
¼ cup butter or margarine, melted
1 (5 ounce) package medium egg noodles
1 (8 ounce) package cream cheese, softened
2 cups (8 ounces) shredded sharp cheddar cheese
1 (10 ounce) package frozen English peas, thawed and drained
1 (2½ ounce) jar mushroom stems and pieces, undrained
½ teaspoon black pepper
10 butter-flavored crackers, crushed

In small skillet, sauté onion and red pepper in butter until tender. Set aside. Cook noodles according to package directions; drain. Add cream cheese and cheddar cheese to hot noodles; stir until cheeses melt. Stir in onion mixture, peas, mushrooms, and pepper. Spoon into greased baking dish and top with cracker crumbs. Cover and bake at 325 degrees for 25 to 30 minutes.

⁕ French-Style Green Beans ⁕

⅔ cup slivered almonds
6 tablespoons butter or margarine
2 (10 ounce) packages frozen french-style green beans, thawed
½ teaspoon salt

In large skillet, sauté almonds in butter until lightly browned, about 1 to 2 minutes. Stir in beans and salt; cook and stir for 1 to 2 minutes or until heated through.

Experience an Inspiring
Christmas at Home. . . .

"Gifts" That Will Make Your Christmas Merrier:
• Forgive and forget.
• Call an old friend to catch up.
• Be thankful for what you do have.
• Make more time for family.
• Laugh.
• Thank God for the Gift of Love He sent for you and me!

Orange–Sweet Potato Casserole

4 large sweet potatoes
½ cup brown sugar, divided
2 tablespoons butter
    or margarine

1 (11 ounce) can mandarin
    oranges, drained
½ cup orange juice

TOPPING:
½ cup chopped walnuts
¼ cup sweetened,
    flaked coconut
1 tablespoon brown sugar

½ teaspoon ground cinnamon
2 tablespoons butter
    or margarine

Boil whole potatoes for 30 to 40 minutes. Cool, then peel
and slice into ¼-inch slices. Arrange half of potato slices in
greased casserole dish. Sprinkle with ¼ cup brown sugar. Dot
with butter. Arrange half of oranges on top. Repeat layers.
Pour orange juice over all. Cover and bake at 350 degrees for
45 minutes. While casserole is baking, mix together walnuts,
coconut, brown sugar, and cinnamon. Cut butter into mixture
and set aside. Remove casserole from oven, uncover, and
sprinkle topping over potatoes. Return to oven uncovered for
10 minutes.

Oyster Corn Bread Dressing

2 (8 ounce) packages
   corn bread mix
4 tablespoons butter
¾ cup chopped onion
3 stalks celery, chopped
2 garlic cloves, minced
2 (8 ounce) cans oysters,
   liquid reserved and
   oysters chopped

2 eggs, beaten
½ teaspoon black pepper
1½ teaspoons ground sage
3 teaspoons poultry seasoning
1 (14 ounce) can chicken stock

Prepare corn bread as instructed on package; allow to cool before crumbling corn bread into large mixing bowl. In large saucepan, melt butter over low heat and sauté onion, celery, garlic, and oysters until onion is glassy and tender. Stir oysters into corn bread crumbs. In separate bowl, beat eggs; then season with pepper, sage, and poultry seasoning. Mix in chicken stock and reserved oyster liquid. Blend egg mixture into corn bread mixture. Place in greased 2-quart casserole dish. Bake uncovered at 350 degrees for 45 minutes.

Candy Apple Salad

2 cups water
¼ cup red cinnamon candies
1 (3 ounce) package cherry gelatin
½ cup chopped celery
1½ cups chopped tart apples
½ cup chopped walnuts

In saucepan, bring water to boil. Add cinnamon candies; stir until dissolved. Remove from heat and add gelatin; stir until dissolved. Cool slightly, then refrigerate until gelatin begins to thicken. Add remaining ingredients; blend well. Pour into 8-inch square dish and chill until firm.

For unto you is born this day in the city of David a Saviour, which is Christ the Lord.
LUKE 2:11 KJV

⸱⸱⸱⸻ Champagne Salad ⸻⸱⸱⸱

1 (8 ounce) package cream cheese, softened
¾ cup sugar
1 (20 ounce) can crushed pineapple, drained
1 (10 ounce) package frozen strawberries, with juice
2 bananas, sliced
½ cup chopped nuts
1 (16 ounce) container frozen whipped topping, thawed

Beat cream cheese with sugar. In separate bowl, mix together pineapple, strawberries with juice, bananas, nuts, and whipped topping. Gently combine with cream cheese mixture. Pour into 9x13-inch pan and freeze completely. To serve, thaw slightly and cut into squares. Keep leftovers frozen.

Christmas Fruit Salad

3 egg yolks, beaten
3 tablespoons water
3 tablespoons white vinegar
½ teaspoon salt
2 cups whipping
  cream, whipped
3 cups miniature
  marshmallows
2 cups seedless green
  grapes, halved

1 (20 ounce) can pineapple
  tidbits, drained
1 (11 ounce) can mandarin
  oranges, drained
1 (10 ounce) jar red
  maraschino cherries,
  drained and sliced
1 cup chopped pecans
3 tablespoons lemon juice

In large saucepan, combine egg yolks, water, vinegar, and salt. Stirring constantly, cook over medium heat until mixture thickens. Remove from heat and fold in whipped cream. In large bowl, mix together remaining ingredients. Add dressing and stir gently to combine. Cover and refrigerate overnight.

Cranberry Salad

1 (3 ounce) package cherry gelatin
1 cup hot water
1 can whole berry cranberry sauce
1 cup sour cream
½ cup chopped pecans

Mix gelatin with hot water. Stir until dissolved. Refrigerate until slightly congealed. Stir in cranberry sauce, sour cream, and pecans. Pour into a mold and refrigerate until completely set.

Layered Broccoli–
Cauliflower Salad

6 slices bacon
1 cup broccoli florets
1 cup cauliflower florets
3 hard-boiled eggs, chopped
½ cup chopped red onion
1 cup mayonnaise

½ cup sugar
2 tablespoons white
  wine vinegar
1 cup shredded
  cheddar cheese

In large skillet, cook bacon over medium-high heat until crispy. Crumble and set aside. In medium glass salad bowl, layer in order broccoli, cauliflower, eggs, and onion. Prepare dressing by whisking together mayonnaise, sugar, and vinegar. Drizzle dressing over top. Sprinkle crumbled bacon and cheese over dressing. Chill completely to blend flavors.

Mandarin Orange Salad

2 cups boiling water
1 (6 ounce) package
 orange gelatin
1 pint orange sherbet

1 (11 ounce) can mandarin
 oranges, drained
1 (8.5 ounce) can crushed
 pineapple, undrained

In mixing bowl, pour boiling water over gelatin. Stir until dissolved. Spoon orange sherbet into gelatin and stir until well combined. Fold in remaining ingredients. Pour into gelatin mold and refrigerate until firm.

Experience an Inspiring Christmas at Home. . . .

Try to recapture the childlike wonder of the season by enjoying the simple pleasures. Build a snowman; have a friendly snowball fight with the kids; go ice skating or sled riding; read a Christmas story in front of a blazing fire; drive around town to view the holiday displays and lights; don't count calories when you're enjoying those holiday treats; and drink LOTS of hot chocolate!

Marinated Vegetable Salad

¾ cup white vinegar
½ cup oil
1 cup sugar
1 teaspoon salt
½ teaspoon black pepper
2 (11 ounce) cans white corn
1 (15 ounce) can small
 sweet peas

1 (15 ounce) can french-
 style green beans
1 cup diced green pepper
1 cup diced celery
1 cup diced onion
1 (2 ounce) jar diced pimiento

In small saucepan, bring vinegar, oil, sugar, salt, and pepper to boil; stir until sugar dissolves. Cool. Combine remaining ingredients in bowl. Stir in vinegar mixture. Chill for 8 hours or overnight. Drain before serving.

Wilted Spinach Salad

8 slices bacon, diced
1 tablespoon brown sugar
⅓ cup thinly sliced
    green onions
Salt to taste

3 tablespoons white vinegar
¼ teaspoon dry mustard
1 pound fresh spinach,
    washed, dried, and chilled
1 hard-boiled egg, chopped

In heavy skillet, fry diced bacon until crisp; reduce heat. Stir in brown sugar, onions, salt, vinegar, and mustard; bring to boil. Pour hot mixture over spinach. Toss lightly. Sprinkle chopped egg over salad. Serve immediately.

Cranberry Waldorf Salad

3 (3 ounce) packages peach gelatin
1¼ teaspoons salt
3 cups boiling water
2 cups cranberry juice cocktail
2 tablespoons lemon juice
1½ cups apples, diced
½ cup nuts, coarsely chopped

Dissolve gelatin and salt in boiling water. Stir in cranberry juice and lemon juice. Chill until slightly thickened. Fold in apples and nuts. Chill until firm. Can be put into 2-quart mold.

Spinach-Stuffed Tomatoes

1 (10 ounce) package frozen chopped spinach
¼ cup water
¼ cup mayonnaise
1 tablespoon dried minced onion
⅛ teaspoon nutmeg
Salt and pepper to taste
6 small whole tomatoes

Cook spinach in water for 3 minutes, stirring to defrost; drain completely. Combine spinach with mayonnaise, onion, nutmeg, salt, and pepper. Cut thin slice off tops of tomatoes and scoop out center; drain upside down. Sprinkle inside of tomatoes with salt and fill with spinach mixture. Place tomatoes in baking dish and pour hot water ¼-inch deep around tomatoes. Bake at 350 degrees for 12 to 15 minutes.

French Rice

1 (10¾ ounce) can onion soup, undiluted
½ cup butter or margarine, melted
1 (4.5 ounce) jar sliced mushrooms
1 (8 ounce) can sliced water chestnuts
1 cup uncooked rice

Preheat oven to 350 degrees. In large bowl, combine soup and butter. Drain mushrooms and water chestnuts, reserving liquid. Add enough water to reserved liquid to equal 1⅓ cups. Add mushrooms, water chestnuts, liquid, and rice to soup mixture; stir well. Pour into lightly greased 10x6x2-inch baking dish. Cover and bake for 1 hour.

Mixed Vegetable Medley

1 (10 ounce) package
frozen peas
1 (10 ounce) package
frozen green beans
1 (10 ounce) package
frozen cauliflower
¾ cup water

1 (2 ounce) jar sliced
pimiento, drained
2 tablespoons margarine
or butter
½ teaspoon dried basil leaves
½ teaspoon salt
⅛ teaspoon pepper

Bring vegetables and water to boil and reduce heat. Cover and cook over low heat about 7 minutes or until vegetables are tender. Drain and stir in remaining ingredients.

Come to Bethlehem
and see Christ whose
birth the angels sing;
Come adore on bended knee,
Christ the Lord,
the newborn King.
Gloria, in excelsis Deo!
Gloria, in excelsis Deo!
TRADITIONAL FRENCH CAROL

Cinnamon Sweet Potatoes

2½ pounds sweet potatoes or yams (7 or 8 medium)
½ cup packed brown sugar
¼ cup margarine or butter
3 tablespoons water
½ teaspoon ground cinnamon
½ teaspoon salt

Heat salted water (½ teaspoon salt to 1 cup water) to boiling. Add potatoes. Cover and bring back to boil, cooking 30 to 35 minutes, or until tender. Drain. Remove skins. Cut potatoes crosswise into ½-inch slices. Combine brown sugar, margarine, water, cinnamon, and salt in 10-inch skillet. Cook over medium heat, stirring constantly until smooth. Add potato slices and stir until glazed and heated through.

Green Peas with Celery and Onion

2 packages (10 ounces each) frozen peas
½ cup sliced celery
1 small onion, thinly sliced
3 tablespoons margarine or butter, softened
¼ teaspoon salt

Following directions on package for peas, cook celery, onion, and peas; drain. Stir in margarine and salt.

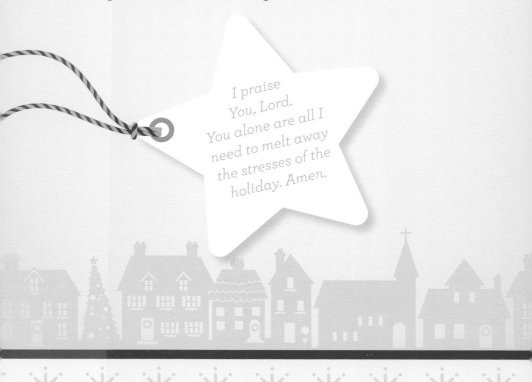

I praise You, Lord. You alone are all I need to melt away the stresses of the holiday. Amen.

Glazed Carrots

1¼ pounds fresh carrots (about 8 medium)
⅓ cup packed brown sugar
2 tablespoons margarine or butter
½ teaspoon salt
½ teaspoon grated orange peel

Cut carrots in sections 2½ inches in length, then into ⅜-inch strips. Bring 1 inch salted water to boil. Add carrots, cover, and bring to boil again. Reduce heat and cook 18 to 20 minutes, or until tender; drain. Combine brown sugar, margarine, salt, and orange peel in 10-inch skillet; stir and cook until bubbly. Add carrots and cook over low heat about 5 minutes, or until carrots are glazed and heated through.

Granny's Corn Bread

2 tablespoons shortening
2 tablespoons butter
1 cup self-rising cornmeal
¾ cup self-rising flour
½ cup sugar
1 cup milk
1 egg
2 tablespoons oil

Put shortening and butter in cool iron skillet. Put in oven at 425 degrees. Mix remaining ingredients in order listed. Pour in hot skillet from oven. Bake 20 to 30 minutes until golden brown.

Old-Fashioned Mashed Potatoes

8 medium potatoes,
    peeled and sliced
1 medium onion, finely
    chopped
Water
½ to ⅔ cup whole
    milk, divided

⅓ cup butter
1½ teaspoons grated
    Parmesan cheese
1 teaspoon salt
¼ teaspoon sugar
Dash pepper

* * * * *

Cook potatoes and onion until tender in enough boiling water
to cover. Drain and mash. Add ½ cup milk and remaining
ingredients. Mix together. Add more milk, if needed, for
desired consistency. Serve hot.

Sweet Potato Casserole

2 large sweet potatoes
3 eggs, beaten
¼ cup melted butter
⅔ cup evaporated milk

TOPPING:
1 cup chopped pecans
½ cup brown sugar
¼ cup flour
2 tablespoons melted butter

Wash, peel, and cut sweet potatoes. Boil for about 25 minutes, until tender. Drain well and mash. Stir in eggs, butter, and evaporated milk. Spoon into baking dish. Combine topping ingredients, and sprinkle evenly over sweet potatoes. Bake at 350 degrees for 40 minutes or until set.

⋯⚜ Willett's Broccoli-Rice Tradition ⚜⋯

1 cup chopped onions
2 tablespoons butter
1 (10.5 ounce) can cream of chicken or mushroom soup
1 teaspoon salt
½ teaspoon ground black pepper
3 cups cooked rice
1 (10 ounce) package frozen chopped broccoli, thawed
2 cups grated cheddar cheese

In large skillet, cook onions in butter until tender crisp.
Add soup, salt, and pepper. Mix all ingredients and put into
buttered 2-quart baking dish. Mix well. Bake at 350 degrees for
35 minutes or until hot and bubbly.

Nana's Baked Beans

1 pound dry navy beans
6 cups cold water
1 teaspoon salt
12 slices bacon

½ cup brown sugar
¼ cup molasses
1 medium onion, chopped
2 teaspoons dry mustard

Rinse beans. Combine beans and water in large saucepan or dutch oven. Cover and bring to boil for 2 minutes. Remove from heat; let stand 1 hour or overnight. Add salt. Simmer partially covered 1 hour or until beans are tender. Drain, reserving liquid. Cut bacon into 1-inch pieces. Combine uncooked bacon, brown sugar, molasses, onion, and dry mustard with beans in dutch oven or 2-quart bean pot. Add 1¾ cups reserved liquid. Bake uncovered at 300 degrees for 5 hours. Add additional water if necessary.

⋅⋅❧ Old-Fashioned Bread Stuffing ❧⋅⋅

½ cup butter
1 cup chopped sweet onion
½ cup chopped celery,
   with leaves
8 cups bread cubes
2 tablespoons hot chicken
   or turkey broth

1 teaspoon salt
¼ teaspoon pepper
1 teaspoon sage
½ teaspoon thyme
½ teaspoon marjoram

Melt butter in frying pan. Add onion and celery, and cook until soft but not browned. Combine butter mixture with bread cubes, broth, and seasonings. For soft, moist dressing, use fresh or slightly stale bread. For lighter, fluffier dressing, use dried, stale bread. Makes enough to stuff an 8- to 10-pound turkey.

> But when the fulness of the time was come, God sent forth his Son.
> GALATIANS 4:4 KJV

❄ Stuffed Winter Squash ❄

3 small acorn or butternut squash
1 large sweet onion, diced
1 tablespoon olive oil
1 cup finely diced celery
1 cup fresh spinach, coarsely chopped
1 cup whole wheat bread crumbs
¼ teaspoon salt
¼ cup finely ground almonds
2 tablespoons butter

Clean squash and cut each in half. Bake at 350 degrees for 35 minutes or until tender. Sauté onion in oil until soft. Add diced celery. Cover and simmer on medium heat until tender. Add spinach; stir to wilt. Combine bread crumbs with salt and ground nuts. Stuff squash halves with spinach mixture and sprinkle crumb mixture on top. Dot with butter. Return to oven for 10 to 15 minutes.

·⊰ Kidney Bean Salad ⊱·

⅓ cup mayonnaise
1 teaspoon prepared mustard
1 medium sweet onion,
   chopped fine
1 cup celery, chopped fine
1 small cucumber, diced
2 (16 ounce) cans red
   kidney beans, drained

4 hard-boiled eggs, cut
   into 8 pieces each
Seasoned salt
Lettuce
Red and green vegetables

Mix mayonnaise, mustard, onion, celery, and cucumber. Fold in drained kidney beans and eggs. Season to taste with seasoned salt. Chill 2 hours until flavors are blended. Serve on lettuce, and garnish with red and green vegetables for Christmas.

Experience an Inspiring Christmas at Home. . . .

Bake up oodles of Christmas cookies and hand-deliver them to your neighbors. Attach signature gift tags. You can find several free gift-tag designs online, print your own tags on holiday labels, or create your own using card stock, colored pens, stamps, and stickers.

Noel's Jellied Salad

1 (20 ounce) can crushed pineapple
Several cups water
1 package lemon jelly powder
½ cup sugar
¼ teaspoon salt
2 tablespoons lemon juice
1 cup finely grated carrots
1 cup whipping cream

Drain pineapple and reserve juice. Set pineapple aside. Mix pineapple juice with enough water to make 1½ cups of liquid. Heat to boil. Stir in jelly powder until dissolved. Mix in sugar, salt, and lemon juice. Remove from heat and chill until slightly thickened. Add reserved pineapple and carrots. Whip cream until stiff and fold into jelly mixture. Pour into jelly mold and chill overnight. Unmold by dipping into shallow bowl of hot water and serve.

Auntie's Bean Salad

1 (16 ounce) can green beans
1 (16 ounce) can wax beans
1 (16 ounce) can lima beans
1 (16 ounce) can chickpeas

½ cup chopped green pepper
½ cup chopped onion
¼ cup chopped pimento

DRESSING:

½ cup vegetable oil
½ cup white wine vinegar
½ cup sugar

2 teaspoons salt
½ teaspoon white pepper
¼ teaspoon black pepper

Mix together beans, green pepper, onion, and pimento. Set aside. Blend dressing ingredients well and pour over bean mixture. Toss. Marinate overnight in refrigerator. Serve cold.

Fresh Cranberry Relish

2 large oranges
4 cups fresh cranberries, washed and stemmed
2 red apples, cored but not pared
2 cups sugar

Peel oranges and reserve half of 1 peel. Chop oranges coarsely. Put cranberries, apples, and reserved peel through coarse blade of food chopper or food processor. Add oranges and sugar; mix well. Refrigerate at least 2 hours before serving.

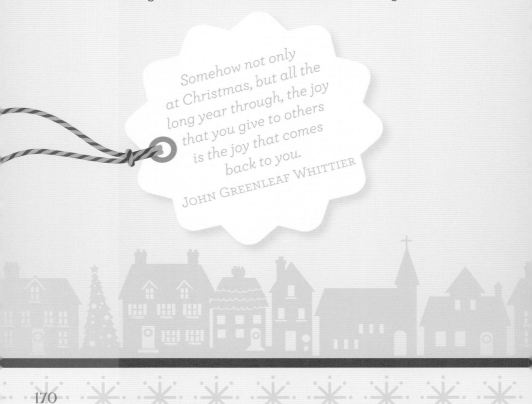

Somehow not only at Christmas, but all the long year through, the joy that you give to others is the joy that comes back to you.

JOHN GREENLEAF WHITTIER

⋅⋅⋇⋅ Make-Ahead Mashed Potatoes ⋅⋇⋅⋅

3 pounds medium-size potatoes, peeled
1½ cups sour cream
5 tablespoons butter or margarine, divided
1½ teaspoons salt
¼ teaspoon pepper
¼ cup bread crumbs

Cook potatoes to boiling in salted water until tender.
Drain well. In large bowl, combine potatoes, sour cream, 4
tablespoons butter, and seasonings. Beat at low speed until
blended; beat at high speed until light and fluffy. Spoon into
lightly greased 2-quart casserole dish. Cover and refrigerate
overnight. Bake covered at 325 degrees for 1 hour. Melt
remaining 1 tablespoon of butter and mix with bread crumbs.
Sprinkle over potatoes. Continue baking uncovered 30
minutes.

Zesty Carrots

6 to 8 carrots, cut into
    ¼-inch slices
½ cup mayonnaise
2 tablespoons minced onion
1 tablespoon prepared
    horseradish
¼ cup shredded
    cheddar cheese

1 teaspoon salt
¼ teaspoon black pepper
½ cup crushed corn flakes
1 tablespoon butter or
    margarine, melted

Place carrots in saucepan and cover with water. Cook for 5 minutes. Drain, reserving ¼ cup water. Pour reserved liquid into mixing bowl. Stir in mayonnaise, onion, horseradish, cheese, salt, and pepper. Mix well. Add carrots. Transfer to greased 2-quart casserole dish. Sprinkle with crushed corn flakes and drizzle with butter. Bake at 350 degrees for 20 to 25 minutes.

Marinated Mushroom–
Spinach Salad

½ cup oil
¼ cup white wine vinegar
1 small onion, sliced
½ teaspoon basil
1 teaspoon salt
¾ teaspoon fresh ground pepper
½ pound mushrooms, washed and sliced thin
1 pound spinach, washed and torn into bite-size pieces

In medium bowl, combine oil, vinegar, onion, basil, salt, and pepper. Add mushrooms. Let stand at room temperature for 2 hours or refrigerate overnight, stirring occasionally. Place spinach in salad bowl; add mushroom-oil mixture and toss well. Serve immediately.

⋅⋅⋅❧ Evergreen Gelatin Salad ❧⋅⋅⋅

1 large box lime gelatin
2 cups boiling water
1 (8 ounce) package cream cheese
1 (15 ounce) can crushed pineapple
1 (12 ounce) container whipped topping

Combine gelatin and boiling water; allow to cool. Combine cream cheese, pineapple, and whipped topping. Add to gelatin mixture. Chill until firm.

Experience an Inspiring Christmas at Home. . . .

Whatever you give to others this Christmas, be sure to give from your heart.

Cauliflower Salad

4 cups raw cauliflower florets
1 cup stuffed green olives, chopped
⅔ cup green pepper, chopped
½ cup onion, chopped
½ cup pimiento (may include ones in stuffed olives)
½ cup salad oil
3 tablespoons lemon juice
3 tablespoons wine vinegar
1 tablespoon salt
½ teaspoon sugar
¼ teaspoon pepper

Combine cauliflower, olives, green pepper, onion, and pimiento. Shake remaining ingredients together to make a dressing and pour over vegetables. Refrigerate 4 hours.

Christmassy Candies & Desserts

*I heard the bells
on Christmas Day
Their old familiar carols play,
And wild and sweet
the words repeat
Of peace on earth,
good will to men.*
HENRY WADSWORTH
LONGFELLOW

⋯⊰ Christmas Twists ⊱⋯

1 cup sour cream
2 tablespoons shortening
3 tablespoons sugar
⅛ teaspoon baking
   soda
1 teaspoon salt
1 large egg
1 package yeast

3 cups flour, sifted
2 tablespoons butter,
   softened
¼ cup packed brown sugar
1 teaspoon cinnamon
Red and green sugar
   for decorating

In saucepan, bring sour cream to boil. Remove from heat and add shortening, sugar, baking soda, and salt. Mix well and allow to cool. Add egg and yeast, stirring until yeast is dissolved. Mix in flour with wooden spoon. Lightly flour cutting board. Knead dough lightly on board until smooth ball is formed. Cover with damp cloth and let stand for 5 minutes to set. Roll dough to ½-inch thickness in a 6x24-inch rectangle. Spread surface with softened butter. Mix together brown sugar and cinnamon. Sprinkle half of dough with sugar mixture down long side of rectangle. Fold unsugared half of dough over sugared half, pressing top lightly to seal. With sharp knife, cut dough into 24 (1-inch) strips. Take each strip of dough at both ends and twist it twice. Place on greased baking sheet. Cover with damp cloth and let rise at room temperature until very light (about 1½ hours). Right before baking, sprinkle with red and green sugar. Bake for 12 to 15 minutes at 375 degrees.

Strawberries Dipped in Chocolate

6 squares white chocolate
6 squares milk chocolate
15 large strawberries
   with stems on

Finely chopped nuts
Flaked coconut

Melt chocolate in microwave. Holding strawberries by stems, dip in chocolate. You can experiment with dipping in one color and then another. Place strawberries on tray or cookie sheet lined with waxed paper. After a few minutes, drizzle with contrast color of chocolate or sprinkle with finely chopped nuts or flaked coconut.

Experience an Inspiring Christmas at Home. . . .

Give the gift of tasty treats from your kitchen this Christmas. After all, who can resist a gift baked with love? Wrap a stack of cookies with red or green plastic wrap and secure with festive ribbon.

Mini Peanut Butter Cheesecakes

2 (8 ounce) packages cream cheese, softened
¾ cup sugar
2 eggs
1 teaspoon vanilla
1 box vanilla wafers
24 chocolate peanut butter cups

Preheat oven to 350 degrees. In bowl, beat cream cheese, sugar, eggs, and vanilla until well mixed and smooth. Place 1 vanilla wafer in each cup of mini cupcake tin. Fill each cup about halfway with cheesecake mixture. Push 1 peanut butter cup into center of each cheesecake. Bake for 15 minutes. Run knife around sides of each cheesecake and allow to cool completely before removing from tin.

···❦ Monkey Bread ❧···

¾ cup sugar
2 tablespoons cinnamon
2 tubes refrigerated biscuits, cut into quarters
¾ cup finely chopped pecans
½ cup butter, melted

Preheat oven to 350 degrees. Mix sugar and cinnamon in resealable plastic bag. Toss biscuit pieces, a few at a time, in sugar mixture until well coated. Place biscuits in greased Bundt pan. Add remaining sugar-cinnamon mixture and pecans to butter and heat until sugar is dissolved. Pour evenly over biscuits. Bake for 25 minutes. Let cool until warm. Invert cake pan on round platter. You can separate monkey bread into individual servings or guests can pull off pieces of bread.

Snowball Candy

½ cup butter
2 tablespoons milk
¾ cup honey
1 cup flour

¼ teaspoon salt
1 teaspoon vanilla
2 cups flaked coconut, divided
2 cups crisp rice cereal

In medium saucepan, melt butter and add milk, honey, flour, and salt. Stir constantly until mixture forms ball. Remove from heat. Stir in vanilla, 1½ cups coconut, and rice cereal. Shape into 1-inch balls and roll in remaining coconut. Refrigerate.

All this took place to fulfill what the Lord had said through the prophet: "The virgin will conceive and give birth to a son, and they will call him Immanuel" (which means "God with us").

MATTHEW 1:22–23 NIV

Holiday Cherry Tartlets

1 cup graham cracker crumbs, finely crushed
3 tablespoons butter, melted
1 (8 ounce) package cream cheese, softened
1 teaspoon vanilla
1 egg
⅓ cup sugar
1 (21 ounce) can cherry pie filling

Preheat oven to 375 degrees. Grease 24 mini tartlet cups or 2 multiple tartlet pans (with approximately 2-inch cups). Mix graham cracker crumbs with butter and press mixture into bottom of cups. With electric mixer, combine cream cheese, vanilla, egg, and sugar until smooth. Fill each cup and bake for about 10 minutes. Remove from oven, cool completely, and allow to set in refrigerator overnight. Before serving, use butter knife to gently lift each tartlet out of pan. Top with small dollop of cherry pie filling.

·⋇· Gingerbread Delight ⋇·

1 (15 ounce) box gingerbread cake mix
½ cup butter, melted
1 cup brown sugar
1 (29 ounce) can pears, drained
Whipped topping for serving

* * * * ⋇ ⋇ ⋇ ⋇ ⋇ * * *

Preheat oven to 350 degrees. Mix gingerbread cake batter
according to box instructions. Pour melted butter in bottom
of 9x13-inch cake pan. Sprinkle brown sugar over butter. Place
pears on top of brown sugar. Pour cake batter over pears. Bake
according to cake mix instructions. Allow cake to cool for
several minutes. Invert onto platter. Serve with whipped cream.

Candy Cane Brownies

4 eggs
2 cups sugar
1 cup butter
3 squares unsweetened
   chocolate
2 cups flour
1 teaspoon vanilla
1 cup crushed candy
   canes

FROSTING:
1 pound powdered sugar
¼ teaspoon peppermint
   extract
Milk
Red food coloring
¼ cup water
2 tablespoons butter
½ teaspoon vanilla
2 squares unsweetened
   chocolate
2 cups powdered sugar

Preheat oven to 350 degrees and grease jelly roll pan. In small bowl, beat eggs; add sugar. In large saucepan, melt butter and chocolate. Cool slightly. Add sugar and egg mixture; then add flour, vanilla, and crushed candy canes. Pour into pan and bake for 20 minutes. Cool completely before frosting.

FROSTING: Combine powdered sugar and peppermint extract with enough milk to make frosting. Mix in a few drops red food coloring. Spread over brownies. In saucepan over low heat, melt water, butter, vanilla, and chocolate. Add enough powdered sugar (up to 2 cups) to make frosting of desired consistency.

Pretzel Wreaths

1 (16 ounce) package white or milk chocolate candy melts
Almond or peppermint extract, if desired
1 bag small pretzel twists
Christmas sprinkles

Melt chocolate, adding a few drops almond or peppermint extract if desired. Dip rounded bottoms of five pretzels into chocolate. Lay pretzels on waxed paper in a circle with sides touching and chocolate edges toward center. Repeat and place second circle on top of first, slightly staggered. Decorate wreath with sprinkles. Allow to cool completely before packaging.

Oatmeal-Cranberry White Chocolate Chunk Cookies

⅔ cup butter
⅔ cup brown sugar
2 eggs
1 teaspoon vanilla
1½ cups flour
1 teaspoon baking soda

½ teaspoon salt
1½ cups oats
¾ cup dried cranberries
⅔ cup white chocolate chunks
⅔ cup chopped walnuts

Preheat oven to 375 degrees. In large bowl, beat butter and brown sugar until light and fluffy. Add eggs and vanilla, mixing well. Combine dry ingredients in separate bowl. Gradually add to butter mixture, mixing well. Stir in cranberries, chocolate chunks, and walnuts. Drop by rounded teaspoonfuls onto ungreased cookie sheet. Bake for 8 to 10 minutes or until golden brown.

Peppermint Bark

1 (16 ounce) package white or dark chocolate candy melts
½ teaspoon peppermint extract
6 candy canes, crushed

Melt chocolate according to package instructions. Add extract and stir. Pour melted chocolate onto cookie sheet lined with waxed paper and spread evenly. Sprinkle candy cane pieces onto chocolate and gently press down. Refrigerate until set. Break into pieces. Store in airtight container in refrigerator.

Gingerbread Fudge

1 cup sugar
1 cup packed light brown
   sugar
¼ cup molasses
¼ cup light corn
   syrup
½ cup whipping
   cream
¼ teaspoon salt
½ teaspoon cream of tartar

2 tablespoons instant
   espresso powder dissolved
   in ¼ cup water
¾ cup dark chocolate,
   finely chopped
1 teaspoon vanilla
¼ teaspoon ginger
¾ teaspoon allspice
3 tablespoons butter

Line 8x8-inch pan with foil and grease with butter. In large saucepan, combine sugars, molasses, corn syrup, cream, salt, cream of tartar, and espresso. Cook over medium heat, stirring constantly until sugar is dissolved (3 to 4 minutes). Remove from heat; stir in chocolate until melted and smooth. Return to heat and cook without stirring until mixture reaches 238 degrees (soft ball stage). Remove from heat and stir in vanilla, spices, and butter. Allow to cool to 110 degrees. Beat until mixture loses sheen and forms peaks. Pour into prepared pan and let stand at room temperature for at least 3 hours. Lift out by corners of foil.

⋯⋅∈ Reindeer Food ∋⋅⋯

10 cups crispy cereal squares
1¼ cups white chocolate chips
½ cup peanut butter
¼ cup butter
½ teaspoon vanilla
1½ cups powdered sugar

Put cereal in large bowl. In saucepan, melt chocolate chips, peanut butter, and butter. Remove from heat and add vanilla. Pour mixture over cereal and toss. Add powdered sugar to bowl and toss until cereal is well coated. Turn out on cookie sheets lined with waxed paper to cool.

Almond Butter Crunch

1½ cups coarsely chopped almonds, divided
½ cup butter or margarine
1½ cups sugar
1 tablespoon light corn syrup
3 tablespoons water
12 ounces melting chocolate wafers

Spread almonds on waxed paper and microwave for 7 to
10 minutes, stirring frequently until lightly toasted. Butter
rimmed cookie sheet. Microwave butter in medium glass dish
for 1½ to 2 minutes. Stir in sugar, corn syrup, and water. Heat
for 12 to 14 minutes until mixture is color of peanut butter (soft
crack stage, 270–290 degrees). Stir in ¾ chopped almonds.
Spread evenly over prepared cookie sheet. When mixture sets
up, melt half of chocolate and spread over one side. Sprinkle
with remaining nuts. When hard, turn over and repeat on other
side.

Chocolate-Covered Pretzels

6 ounces dark chocolate candy melts
6 ounces milk chocolate candy melts
6 ounces white chocolate candy melts
2 large packages pretzel rods
Christmas sprinkles
Mini candy-covered chocolate pieces
Chopped nuts

Melt three types of chocolate in separate bowls in microwave.
Dip pretzel rods in chocolate of choice and place on cookie
sheet lined with waxed paper. Allow to set for a few minutes.
Dip or roll each pretzel rod in topping of choice (sprinkles,
candy-covered chocolate pieces, or nuts). You can also
dip pretzels in dark chocolate and then drizzle with white
chocolate. Use your imagination to create festive goodies.

⸰⸰❧ Frozen Fruit Cake ❧⸰⸰

1 (16 ounce) can cranberry
    sauce, stirred
1 cup miniature
    marshmallows
½ cup sugar

1 (20 ounce) can crushed
    pineapple, drained
½ cup chopped nuts
2 bananas, mashed

Mix all ingredients and pour into oblong pan or mold. Freeze, cut, and serve.

Enjoy an Inspiring Christmas at Home. · · · ·

Host a Christmas cookie-baking marathon. Invite family and friends to bring ingredients for a variety of cookies. Spend all afternoon baking and decorating. Send each participant home with a platter filled with your yummy creations. Definitely more fun—and simpler—than doing all the work yourself!

Remarkable Fudge

4 cups sugar
2 (5 ounce) cans evaporated milk
1 cup butter
1 (7 ounce) jar marshmallow crème
1 cup milk chocolate chips
1 teaspoon vanilla
1 cup chopped nuts, if desired
2 cups semisweet chocolate chips

Line 9x13-inch baking pan with foil, extending foil over edges of pan. Butter foil; set pan aside. Butter sides of large, heavy saucepan. Combine sugar, milk, and butter in saucepan. Cook and stir over medium-high heat until mixture boils. Reduce heat to medium; continue cooking for 10 minutes, stirring constantly. Remove pan from heat. Add remaining ingredients and stir until chocolate melts. Beat by hand for 1 minute. Spread in prepared pan. Score into 1-inch pieces while still warm. When fudge is firm, use foil to lift out of pan. Cut fudge into squares. Store in tightly covered container in refrigerator.

···⊰ Candy Apples ⊱···

2 cups sugar
⅔ cup light corn syrup
1 cup water
¼ teaspoon cinnamon
Red food coloring, if desired
5 medium apples, with wooden skewers
    inserted in stem end of each

In saucepan, combine sugar, corn syrup, water, and cinnamon. Cook, stirring constantly, over medium heat until sugar is dissolved. Bring to boil. Cover and cook for 3 minutes until steam has washed away any crystals on sides of pan. Uncover and cook without stirring until candy thermometer reads 290 degrees. Remove from heat. Pour into top of double boiler over hot but not boiling water. Add a few drops of red food coloring if desired. Working quickly, dip each apple in candy mixture. Turn apples to coat thoroughly. Scrape off excess candy. Stand apples on waxed paper. Allow to harden.

Sugarplums

½ cup white chocolate
chips
¼ cup light corn
syrup
½ cup chopped dates

¼ cup chopped
maraschino cherries
1 teaspoon vanilla
1¼ cups crushed gingersnaps
Flaked coconut

In small saucepan, melt chocolate chips with corn syrup, stirring constantly. Stir in dates, cherries, and vanilla. Blend well. Add gingersnaps, stirring until blended. Mixture will be stiff. Form mixture into ¾-inch balls and roll in coconut. Place in small foil cups. Let stand overnight to allow flavors to blend.

Chocolate-Covered Cherries

2½ cups semisweet chocolate chips, divided
1 tablespoon butter
36 maraschino cherries with juice

In small saucepan over low heat, melt chocolate chips
with butter, stirring constantly. Spoon about ½ tablespoon
chocolate mixture into 36 small foil cups. With back of spoon,
spread chocolate up sides of each cup, forming hollow center.
Refrigerate until firm. Place 1 cherry and a little juice in each
chocolate cup. Cover with melted chocolate. Refrigerate until
firm. Store in refrigerator.

*What I'd like
to have for Christmas I
can tell you in a minute:
the family all around
me and the home
with laughter in it.*
EDGAR E. GUEST

Velvet Taffy

1 cup molasses
3 cups sugar
1 cup boiling water
3 tablespoons
   vinegar

½ teaspoon cream of tartar
½ cup melted butter
¼ teaspoon baking soda
Powdered sugar

In saucepan, combine molasses, sugar, water, and vinegar. Bring to boil. Add cream of tartar. Stirring constantly, boil until candy thermometer reaches 248 degrees. Add butter and baking soda. Remove from heat. Stir to blend thoroughly. Pour onto cutting board covered with powdered sugar. When cool enough to handle, pull until candy is light colored. Roll into 1-inch diameter rope. Allow to cool. Cut into 1-inch pieces.

Snickerdoodles

½ cup shortening
½ cup butter,
  softened
1½ cups sugar
2 eggs
3 cups flour
2 teaspoons cream of tartar

1 teaspoon baking soda
¼ teaspoon salt

CINNAMON MIXTURE:
2 tablespoons sugar
2 teaspoons cinnamon

In large bowl, mix shortening, butter, sugar, and eggs. In separate bowl, combine dry ingredients and add to creamed mixture. Shape dough into 1-inch balls and roll in cinnamon mixture. Bake at 375 degrees for 10 minutes.

Butterscotch Caramels

1 cup butter, cut into pieces
2½ cups light brown sugar
½ cup dark corn syrup
¼ cup light corn syrup
1 cup heavy cream
2 teaspoons vanilla

In saucepan over low heat, stir butter, brown sugar, and both corn syrups until sugar is dissolved. Bring to boil over medium heat and cook until candy thermometer reaches 248 degrees. Remove from heat. With wooden spoon, gradually add cream. Over medium heat, bring mixture back to boil. Cook until candy thermometer reaches 248 degrees. Remove from heat. Stir in vanilla. Pour into buttered 9x13-inch pan. Let stand until set. When cool, cut into pieces.

Haystacks

1½ cups peanut butter
3 cups butterscotch chips
1 cup pretzel sticks

Melt peanut butter and butterscotch chips over low heat. Remove from heat. Pour over pretzel sticks. Stir to coat. Drop by teaspoonfuls onto waxed paper. Cool.

Experience an Inspiring Christmas at Home. . . .

Step out in faith and trust God to provide for all your needs this Christmas. If your needs seem too great, remember that the Lord likes to surprise us in big ways. Talk to God; He's listening!

Caramel Popcorn

¼ cup butter
½ cup light corn syrup
1 cup brown sugar
⅔ cup sweetened condensed milk
1 teaspoon vanilla
5 cups popped corn, unpopped hulls removed

Combine butter, corn syrup, and brown sugar. Bring to boil.
Stir in condensed milk and return to boil, stirring constantly.
Remove from heat and stir in vanilla. Pour over popped corn
and stir to coat. With buttered hands, form into balls. Place on
waxed paper to set.

Toffee

1 cup pecan pieces
1½ cups brown sugar
1 cup butter
1 teaspoon vanilla

Spread pecan pieces on buttered baking sheet. Set aside.
In saucepan, cook brown sugar and butter until candy
thermometer reads 290 degrees. Remove from heat and stir in
vanilla. Pour over pecan pieces. Let cool completely. Break into
pieces.

Peanut Brittle

1½ cups salted peanuts
1 cup sugar
1 cup light corn syrup
¼ cup water
2 tablespoons butter
¼ teaspoon baking soda

Place peanuts in ungreased 8x8-inch pan and warm in oven at 250 degrees. In saucepan, combine sugar, corn syrup, water, and butter. Stir over medium heat until sugar is dissolved and temperature reaches 280 degrees. Gradually stir in warm peanuts. Keep cooking until temperature reaches 300 degrees, stirring frequently. Remove from heat. Stir in baking soda until thoroughly blended. Pour onto heavily buttered cookie sheet. Spread evenly. Cool about 30 minutes or until set. Break into pieces.

Eggnog Candy

2 cups sugar
¾ cup eggnog
2 tablespoons light corn syrup
2 tablespoons butter
1 teaspoon vanilla

In saucepan over medium heat, cook sugar, eggnog, corn syrup, and butter, stirring constantly until sugar dissolves. Boil until candy thermometer reads 238 degrees. Pour into bowl. Cool to about 110 degrees. Add vanilla and beat with mixer until thick. Spread into buttered 8x8-inch pan. Score into squares. Refrigerate until firm. Store in refrigerator.

Bessie's Sugar Cookies

3 eggs, beaten
2 teaspoons vanilla
2 cups sugar
1 cup lard or shortening
1 cup milk
½ teaspoon baking soda
7 cups flour (approximately)
4 teaspoons baking powder

In large bowl, mix eggs, vanilla, sugar, and lard until smooth. In separate bowl, blend milk and baking soda together; add to egg mixture. In another bowl, sift together flour and baking powder, then slowly add to egg mixture until dough is the right texture for handling. Roll dough out on floured surface and cut into shapes with cookie cutters. Bake at 350 degrees for 10 minutes.

Date Nut Pinwheels

1 cup brown sugar
1 cup sugar
1 cup butter,
   softened
3 eggs
4 cups flour
1 teaspoon baking soda
1 teaspoon baking powder

FILLING:
½ cup sugar
½ cup water
1 pound dates, finely chopped
1 cup walnuts, chopped

In large bowl, cream together sugars and butter. Add eggs and beat well. In separate bowl, sift together flour, baking soda, and baking powder, then blend with creamed mixture. Chill. Roll out to ¼-inch-thick rectangle. Prepare filling by combining sugar and water in saucepan. Add dates and boil over low heat until thick, stirring constantly. Cool. Add nuts. Spread filling over dough. Roll dough lengthwise to form a log. Cover in plastic wrap and chill. When ready to bake, cut ¼-inch slices. Bake at 350 degrees until lightly browned, about 10 minutes.

Frosted Drop Cookies

½ cup shortening
1½ cups brown sugar
1 teaspoon vanilla
2 eggs
2½ cups flour

1 teaspoon baking soda
½ teaspoon baking powder
½ teaspoon salt
1 cup sour cream
½ cup walnuts, chopped

In large bowl, thoroughly cream shortening, sugar, and vanilla. Beat in eggs. In separate bowl, sift together dry ingredients and add to shortening mixture alternately with sour cream. Stir in nuts. Drop by teaspoonfuls onto greased cookie sheet. Bake at 350 degrees for 10 to 12 minutes. Frost with Butter Icing (recipe on page 209).

Butter Icing

6 tablespoons butter
2 cups powdered sugar
1 teaspoon vanilla
Hot water

In saucepan, heat butter until golden brown. Remove from heat and beat in powdered sugar and vanilla. Add enough hot water until mixture is spreading consistency.

Experience an Inspiring Christmas at Home....

Uplift the spirits of your friends and coworkers with this inexpensive Christmas gift idea: pick out an assortment of holiday-shaped cookie cutters—stars, snowmen, Christmas trees, wreaths—and use red and green ribbon to attach a great recipe for cutout cookies.

Anise Drops

4 eggs
1¼ cups sugar
3 cups sifted flour
1¼ tablespoons lightly crushed anise seeds

Beat eggs with sugar until very thick and almost white. Add flour gradually and blend well after each addition. Stir in anise seeds. Warm cookie sheet in oven, lightly butter and then chill until completely cold. Drop dough onto cookie sheet, leaving 1 inch between cookies. Allow to dry uncovered at room temperature overnight. Bake in preheated 300 degree oven for about 20 minutes, or until pale golden.

Every good and perfect gift is from above.
JAMES 1:17 NIV

⋅⋅⋅⊰ Peanut Butter Thumbprints ⊱⋅⋅⋅

1 stick unsalted butter,
   softened
½ cup peanut butter
1¼ cups sugar

1 egg
2 tablespoons milk
2 cups flour
⅔ cup raspberry jam

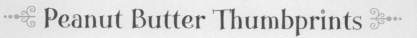

Beat together butter and peanut butter. Add sugar and beat until fluffy; then beat in egg and milk. Add flour, stirring with spoon until thick dough is formed. Place in small, covered bowl and refrigerate at least 2 hours or until well chilled. Preheat oven to 350 degrees. Roll dough into 1-inch balls and place 2 inches apart on buttered cookie sheet. Gently flatten balls with palm of your hand and make small indentation in each with thumb tip. Fill each indentation with ½ teaspoon of jam. Bake for 13 to 15 minutes, or until edges are lightly browned.

French Christmas Cookies

½ cup butter or other shortening (softened)
¾ cup sugar
½ cup honey
2 egg yolks
¼ cup milk
1 teaspoon vanilla
3 cups sifted cake flour

Cream butter and sugar together until light. Add honey and egg yolks, beating well after each addition. Add milk and vanilla. Add flour in small amounts until well blended. Chill dough for 2 hours. Roll to ⅛-inch thick on lightly floured board. Cut into desired shapes and bake on ungreased cookie sheets for 10 minutes at 375 degrees. Cool and frost.

Cheese Danish

2 tubes of crescent rolls
2 (8 ounce) packages cream
  cheese, softened
1 teaspoon vanilla

½ cup white sugar
1 stick butter or margarine
1 teaspoon cinnamon
½ cup brown sugar

Put 1 package of rolls on ungreased 9x13-inch pan. Pat seams closed. Beat cream cheese, vanilla, and white sugar until smooth. Spread over rolls. Place second package of crescent rolls on top. Melt butter with cinnamon and pour over top. Sprinkle with brown sugar and bake in 350 degree oven for 30 to 35 minutes.

Butter Cookies

3 cups flour
1 teaspoon baking powder
½ teaspoon salt
1 cup butter
¾ cup sugar

1 egg
2 tablespoons sour cream
1½ teaspoons vanilla
Decorative sugars

Mix flour, baking powder, and salt. Set aside. Cream butter and sugar. Add egg, sour cream, and vanilla. Blend in dry ingredients. Roll in decorative sugars and cut. Bake at 400 degrees for 5 to 8 minutes.

Take time this Christmastide to go a little way apart, And with the help of God prepare the house that is in your heart.
UNKNOWN

Oatmeal Cookies

1 cup raisins
1 cup water
¾ cup shortening
1½ cups sugar
2 eggs
1 teaspoon vanilla
2½ cups flour

½ teaspoon baking powder
1 teaspoon salt
1 teaspoon baking soda
1 teaspoon cinnamon
½ teaspoon cloves
2 cups rolled oats
¼ cup chopped nuts

In medium saucepan, simmer raisins and water over low heat until raisins are plump, about 20 to 30 minutes. Drain raisin liquid into measuring cup, adding enough water to make ½ cup. Cream shortening, sugar, eggs, and vanilla. Stir in raisin liquid. Sift together flour, baking powder, salt, baking soda, and spices and add to mixture. Add rolled oats, nuts, and raisins. Drop by rounded teaspoonfuls 2 inches apart onto ungreased baking sheet. Bake for 8 to 10 minutes at 400 degrees.

⋅⋅⋅⧉ Sour Cream Cookies ⧉⋅⋅⋅

¼ cup shortening
¼ cup butter, softened
1 cup sugar
1 egg
1 teaspoon vanilla
2⅔ cups flour

1 teaspoon baking powder
½ teaspoon baking soda
½ teaspoon salt
¼ teaspoon nutmeg
½ cup sour cream

In mixing bowl, cream shortening, butter, sugar, egg, and vanilla. Add flour, baking powder, baking soda, salt, and nutmeg. Gradually add sour cream. Mix well. Roll to ¼-inch thick; sprinkle with sugar, and cut with floured cutter. Bake 8 to 10 minutes at 425 degrees.

Pa's Peanut Butter Cookies

2½ cups flour
1 teaspoon baking
  powder
1 teaspoon baking
  soda
¼ teaspoon salt

1 cup butter
1 cup peanut butter
1 cup sugar
1 cup brown sugar
2 eggs
1 teaspoon vanilla

Stir together first 4 ingredients and set aside. Beat butter and peanut butter until smooth. Beat in sugars, eggs, and vanilla. Add flour mixture. If necessary, chill dough. Shape in 1-inch balls, and bake on ungreased cookie sheet at 350 degrees for 12 minutes.

Experience an Inspiring Christmas at Home. . . .

Add a little happy to your holiday. When you find yourself feeling overly stressed this Christmas, curl up in your favorite chair with a steaming mug of coffee and a slice of pie, and read through your favorite portion of scripture. You'll be more joyful for it!

⋅⋅❦ Crunchy Christmas Cookies ❧⋅⋅

1 cup flour
½ teaspoon baking soda
¼ teaspoon baking powder
¼ teaspoon salt
½ cup butter or
    margarine, softened
½ cup brown sugar, packed
1 large egg, lightly beaten

1 teaspoon vanilla
1 cup old-fashioned oats
1 cup corn flakes
½ cup sweetened,
    flaked coconut
½ cup coarsely
    chopped pecans

In small bowl, combine flour, baking soda, baking powder, and salt; set aside. In large mixing bowl, cream butter and brown sugar until light and fluffy. Add egg and vanilla and beat well. Stir in flour mixture just until mixed. Stir in oats, corn flakes, coconut, and pecans. Shape dough into 1-inch balls; place 2 inches apart on lightly greased cookie sheets. Bake at 350 degrees for 10 to 12 minutes. Transfer to wire racks to cool completely.

Index

Festive Appetizers & Finger Foods

Bountiful Beverages

Merry Main Dishes

Seasonal Sides & Salads

Christmassy Candies & Desserts